United States Government Accountability Office

GAO

Report to the Chairman, Subcommittee on Oversight of Government Management, the Federal Workforce, and the District of Columbia, Committee on Homeland Security and Governmental Affairs, United States Senate

January 2012

EMBASSY MANAGEMENT

State Department and Other Agencies Should Further Explore Opportunities to Save Administrative Costs Overseas

GAO

Accountability ★ Integrity ★ Reliability

GAO
Accountability * Integrity * Reliability

Highlights

Highlights of GAO-12-317, a report to the Chairman, Subcommittee on Oversight of Government Management, the Federal Workforce, and the District of Columbia, Committee on Homeland Security and Governmental Affairs, United States Senate

EMBASSY MANAGEMENT

State Department and Other Agencies Should Further Explore Opportunities to Save Administrative Costs Overseas

Why GAO Did This Study

The U.S. government employs more than 23,500 Americans overseas at more than 250 diplomatic and consular posts. These posts require a variety of support services, such as building maintenance and vehicle operations. Agencies may obtain these services, primarily from the Department of State (State), through the International Cooperative Administrative Support Services (ICASS), but participation in most services is voluntary. A 2004 GAO report found that ICASS had not eliminated duplication of support services and that customers generally approved of the quality of ICASS services, but that the level of satisfaction was difficult to quantify.

For this report, GAO assessed (1) how changes in ICASS participation have affected the duplication and cost of support services and (2) customer satisfaction with the quality of ICASS services. GAO surveyed ICASS customers, analyzed ICASS data, interviewed officials from State and seven other agencies, and conducted fieldwork in four countries.

What GAO Recommends

Congress may wish to consider requiring agencies to participate in ICASS services unless they provide a business case to show that they can obtain these services outside of ICASS without increasing overall costs to the U.S. government or that their mission cannot be achieved within ICASS. GAO is also making recommendations regarding the reengineering of administrative processes, use of non-State ICASS service providers, and improvement of service standards. State and U.S. Agency for International Development generally concur.

View GAO-12-317. For more information, contact Michael Courts at (202) 512-8980 or courtsm@gao.gov.

What GAO Found

Agencies continue to provide potentially duplicative administrative services overseas despite slight increases in their participation in ICASS since 2004. When agencies had a choice to opt out of ICASS and provide services independently, they did so about one-third of the time, on average, in 2011. The U.S. Agency for International Development (USAID), however, has reduced duplicative administrative operations by increasing its participation in ICASS markedly since 2005. Agencies have cited several factors for opting out of ICASS, principally concerns about cost, but they do not usually provide any formal rationale to ICASS management and often have not conducted any cost analysis to justify their decisions. Some agencies also indicated that they cannot meet their mission requirements within ICASS. GAO's analysis of ICASS cost and workload data shows that significant economies of scale can be achieved through greater participation in ICASS. Thus, while agencies may opt out of ICASS because they believe they can obtain less costly services on their own, doing so may actually increase the overall cost to the U.S. government. ICASS management's ability to convince agencies that participating will save them or the U.S. government money is hampered by the lack of comparative cost data to demonstrate potential savings. In 2004, GAO recommended that the ICASS Executive Board—the highest level policy-making body in the ICASS system composed of customer agency representatives—encourage greater ICASS participation. However, experience has shown that board members do not necessarily have the incentive to require their agencies to participate in ICASS, especially if they are unconvinced that it is in their agencies' individual financial interest. In this context, Congressional action may be necessary to increase participation and achieve greater economies of scale. Separately, State has made limited progress improving the cost effectiveness of ICASS services in other ways, such as reducing the need for American staff overseas or using other qualified agencies, such as USAID, to provide some ICASS services.

Results from annual ICASS customer satisfaction surveys as well as GAO's own survey show overall satisfaction with ICASS services. For example, data from the annual ICASS survey indicate that, on a scale from 1 to 5, the average overall score increased from 3.95 in 2005 to 4.03 in 2011. Data from GAO's survey show that nearly 80 percent of agency representatives participating in ICASS indicated that the quality of services was "good" or better. Nonetheless, some dissatisfaction persists, potentially hampering participation. In some cases, performance problems and service limitations could affect agencies' ability to achieve their missions efficiently and effectively. For example, USAID officials have cited the unavailability of ICASS motor pool vehicles for travel to distant project sites as a major impediment to achieving their mission. State's service delivery data suggest that these concerns have merit, as ICASS service providers fulfilled about 70 percent of the requests for non-local transportation in 2011. State has implemented new monitoring tools to improve ICASS managers' ability to evaluate performance, but they do not address some agencies' concerns involving billing errors, inequity, and problems with certain critical services.

_____ United States Government Accountability Office

Contents

Tables

Figures

Abbreviations

AFSA	American Foreign Service Association
Commerce	Department of Commerce
DHS	Department of Homeland Security
DOD	Department of Defense
DOJ	Department of Justice
FAS	Foreign Agricultural Service
HHS	Department of Health and Human Services
ICASS	International Cooperative Administrative Support Services
M/PRI	Office of Management, Policy, Rightsizing, and Innovation
State	Department of State
USAID	U.S. Agency for International Development
USDA	U.S. Department of Agriculture

United States Government Accountability Office
Washington, DC 20548

January 31, 2012

The Honorable Daniel K. Akaka
Chairman
Subcommittee on Oversight of Government
Management, the Federal Workforce,
and the District of Columbia
Committee on Homeland Security
   and Governmental Affairs
United States Senate

Dear Mr. Chairman:

The U.S. government employs more than 23,500 Americans overseas, including nearly 15,000 with the Department of State (State), at more than 250 diplomatic and consular posts. The operation of these posts requires a wide variety of administrative support services for overseas personnel, such as building maintenance, vehicle operations, and travel services, among others. Agencies may obtain these services through the International Cooperative Administrative Support Services (ICASS) system, the principal means by which the U.S. government provides and shares the cost of common services. ICASS is an interagency system established in 1997 for distributing the cost of administrative services at overseas posts and is intended to ensure that each agency bears the cost of its overseas presence.[1] While State has the primary responsibility for operating the system, over 40 agencies share the cost of ICASS services, which totaled more than $2 billion in fiscal year 2011. State, the Department of Defense (DOD), and the U.S. Agency for International Development (USAID) were the largest participants in ICASS in fiscal year 2010, together accounting for nearly 90 percent of all ICASS costs. The ICASS system seeks to provide quality services at the lowest cost, while ensuring that each agency bears the cost of its presence overseas.

---

[1]The Omnibus Consolidated Appropriations Act of 1997 (Pub. L. No. 104-208) mandated the establishment of a system "that allocates to each department and agency the full cost of its presence outside of the United States." In addition, ICASS operates under various sections of legislation, including provisions authorizing State to enter into agreements with other agencies under certain conditions to consolidate administrative platforms and provide goods and services to other agencies on a reimbursable basis. The *Foreign Affairs Handbook* also provides guidance on ICASS, including its organization, cost distribution system, and budget and billing process.

GAO-12-317 Embassy Management

However, participation in most ICASS services is voluntary, and agencies may choose to obtain these services outside of ICASS.

In 2004, we reviewed the performance of ICASS for the first time since its implementation.[2] In that report, we found that ICASS had not eliminated costly duplication of administrative support services or achieved economies of scale, systematic cost-containment measures, and the streamlining of operations. We also found that agencies deciding to obtain services outside of ICASS rarely made a business case to explain their decisions. In addition, we found that agencies generally approve of the quality of ICASS services, but the level of satisfaction was difficult to quantify. More recently, officials at some agencies, notably USAID, have expressed serious concerns about the quality of ICASS services.

In March 2011, we issued our first annual report to Congress in response to a new statutory requirement that we identify federal programs, agencies, offices, and initiatives, either within departments or governmentwide, which have duplicative goals or activities.[3] We considered "duplication" to occur when two or more agencies or programs are engaged in the same activities or provide the same services to the same beneficiaries. However, determining whether and to what extent programs are actually duplicative requires programmatic information that is often not readily available. In instances in this report where we lacked such information, we use the term "potential duplication."

This report updates our 2004 report and assesses (1) how changes in ICASS participation have affected the duplication and cost of administrative support services and (2) customer satisfaction with the quality of ICASS services overseas. To address these objectives, we reviewed legislation governing ICASS; analyzed data and documentation on ICASS participation, costs, and performance metrics from 2000 through 2011;[4] reviewed the results of annual ICASS surveys; and

---

[2]GAO, *Embassy Management: Actions Are Needed to Increase Efficiency and Improve Delivery of Administrative Support Services*, GAO-04-511 (Washington, D.C.: Sept. 7, 2004).

[3]GAO, *Opportunities to Reduce Potential Duplication in Government Programs, Save Tax Dollars, and Enhance Revenue*, GAO-11-318SP (Washington, D.C.: Mar. 1, 2011).

[4]We assessed the reliability of these data and determined that they were sufficiently reliable for the purposes of our report.

interviewed cognizant staff at State, USAID, DOD, and five other agencies with a large overseas presence: the Departments of Agriculture (USDA), Commerce (Commerce), Health and Human Services (HHS), Homeland Security (DHS), and Justice (DOJ). Together, these eight agencies accounted for more than 98 percent of the total ICASS budget in 2010. We also surveyed representatives from these agencies at posts around the world regarding their agencies' participation in ICASS and their opinions about the cost and quality of ICASS services.[5] We conducted fieldwork at four overseas locations—Tokyo, Japan; Nairobi, Kenya; Manila, the Philippines; and Kigali, Rwanda—where we observed administrative services, met with embassy management officials, and conducted focus groups of ICASS customers. Appendix I provides more details about our objectives, scope, and methodology.

We conducted this performance audit from August 2010 to January 2012 in accordance with generally accepted government auditing standards. Those standards require that we plan and perform the audit to obtain sufficient, appropriate evidence to provide a reasonable basis for our findings and conclusions based on our audit objectives. We believe that the evidence obtained provides a reasonable basis for our findings and conclusions based on our audit objectives.

Background

Under State's leadership, ICASS relies on collaboration among multiple agencies both in Washington, D.C., and at overseas posts to develop and implement ICASS policies. The following bodies have a role in implementing the ICASS system:

- In Washington, D.C., the ICASS Executive Board sets the strategic vision for ICASS and is the highest level policy-making body in the ICASS system. The board is comprised of senior representatives from participating agencies and is chaired by State.

---

[5]We surveyed a random sample of 350 ICASS Council representatives from the eight agencies within the scope of our review at 133 posts worldwide regarding their agencies' participation in and opinions regarding nine ICASS services. These services were: household furniture, furnishings, and appliance pools; motor pool; shipping and customs; government-owned/long and short-term lease residential building operations; vouchering; leasing; information management technical support; procurement; and human resources for locally engaged staff. We received responses from 184 representatives at 102 posts.

- The ICASS Working Group is the staff arm of the Executive Board responsible for presenting policy issues to the board, making policy decisions when delegated to do so by the board, and resolving issues raised by posts. The Working Group is open to any agency that receives ICASS services.

- The ICASS Service Center, housed within State, serves as the Secretariat to the Executive Board and Working Group. The Service Center is primarily responsible for overseeing worldwide ICASS operations and facilitates and coordinates the ICASS budget and allotments process.

- At overseas posts, the ICASS Council develops local policies on what services will be available at post, selects service providers, and approves the post's ICASS budget. The post ICASS Council consists of representatives from each agency that receives ICASS services at that post.

- The ICASS service provider at overseas posts is responsible for delivering services to customer agencies. While there may be different providers for different services at a given post, State is the principal—and most often only—service provider at most posts around the world. At some posts, USAID provides ICASS services to other agencies as an alternate ICASS service provider in lieu of State.

In addition to these ICASS entities, State and USAID established a Joint Management Board in 2011 to facilitate the continued consolidation of their support services.[6]

Agencies may obtain administrative support from ICASS by participating on a case-by-case basis in each service or group of services available at an overseas post (appendix II lists these services and provides a brief

---

[6]In 2006, we reported on State's and USAID's initial efforts to consolidate overseas support services and found that the two agencies had directed overseas posts to begin the process of identifying duplicative services and initiating further consolidation efforts. See GAO, *Overseas Presence: State and USAID Should Adopt a Comprehensive Plan to Improve the Consolidation of Overseas Support Services*, GAO-06-829 (Washington, D.C.: Sept. 8, 2006). Appendix III provides more details on the status of State-USAID consolidation.

description of each).[7] Agencies may opt out of most services by providing these services for themselves or obtaining them from another source. The ICASS Executive Board has made some services mandatory in most cases for all agencies overseas: these include several services that can only be obtained by the embassy, such as securing diplomatic credentials from the host country, and services provided by the Community Liaison Office at each post, such as providing welcoming and orientation materials and assisting family members with employment opportunities.[8] The ICASS Working Group has further decided that starting in fiscal year 2013, participation in two additional services—security and health services—will be mandatory. All remaining services are optional. Depending on the service, ICASS distributes costs among customers either on the basis of static measures, such as an agency's head count or the space it occupies, or on the amount of service the agency actually uses, such as the number of kilometers driven. When an agency chooses to withdraw from an ICASS service, its share of the fixed cost of that service is reallocated among remaining participants, potentially increasing these agencies' costs. The withdrawing agency must then provide the service itself at its own expense.

Spending on administrative services for agencies overseas through ICASS has increased significantly over the last decade, from $736 million in 2001 to more than $2 billion in 2011 (see fig. 1). Agencies that do not fully participate in ICASS also incur costs to obtain administrative services overseas, but these costs are not always clearly and consistently accounted for by the agencies. According to ICASS officials, several factors explain the growth in spending on services overseas, some of which apply equally to ICASS and non-ICASS services. Since 2001, the increase in U.S. personnel overseas, the addition of new services into ICASS, the construction of new embassy compounds (which are more

---

[7]These groups of services are referred to as "cost centers" in ICASS. For simplicity, in this report we use the term "service" to denote both cost centers and the services provided within those cost centers. Overall, ICASS is implemented in one of two manners: "Standard" and "Lite." An ICASS Standard post breaks the services into 31 cost centers, while an ICASS Lite maintains 16 cost centers. In general, ICASS Lite tends to be used at small posts because the management burden is lower than at ICASS Standard posts. ICASS Standard, however, allows for greater flexibility to customers in choosing which services they will take and avoiding paying for services they do not receive.

[8]These services are mandatory for every agency at post with U.S. direct hire and certain authorized third country national, U.S. contractor, or other staff. At posts where an agency has only local staff, the agency is not required to participate in these services.

costly to maintain than the buildings they replaced), the strengthening of security requirements, and exchange rate fluctuations have all contributed to the increase in the overall spending on administrative services abroad. When these factors are accounted for, per capita costs for ICASS services have remained relatively constant since 2000, according to analysis by the ICASS Service Center.

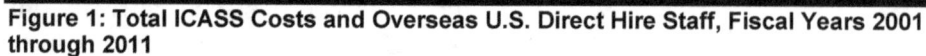

Figure 1: Total ICASS Costs and Overseas U.S. Direct Hire Staff, Fiscal Years 2001 through 2011

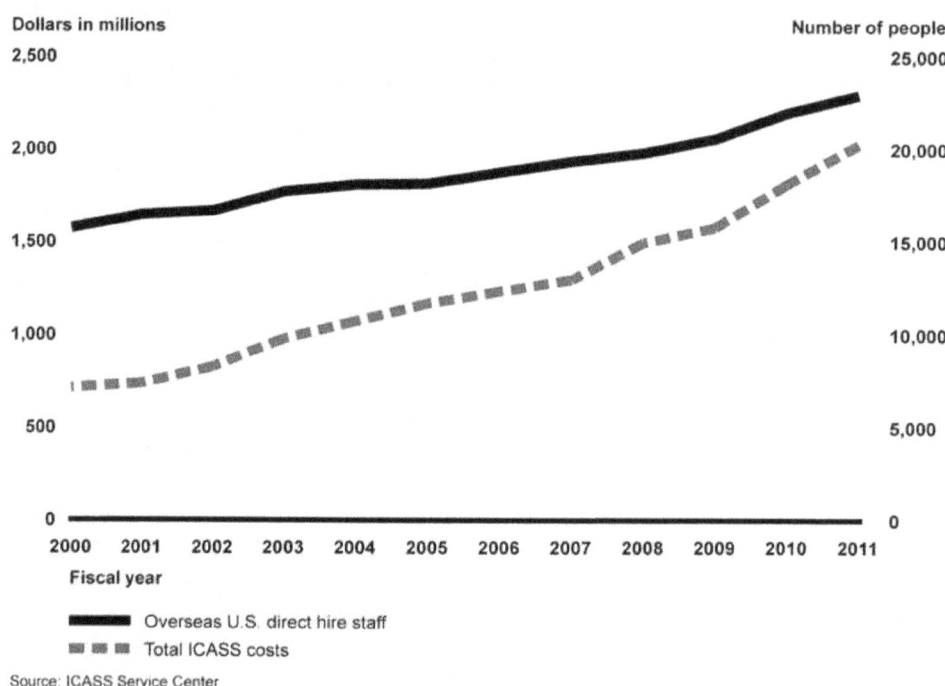

Source: ICASS Service Center

By Opting Out of ICASS Services, Agencies Are Not Realizing Economies of Scale

Since 2004, overall participation in ICASS has increased slightly, but our analysis and observations suggest that agencies are still providing potentially duplicative services at posts overseas. While agencies cite several factors for not participating more fully in ICASS, they generally do not provide justifications for their decisions to opt out of these services. As a result, the government as a whole may be missing opportunities for cost savings resulting from economies of scale within ICASS—that is, the cost per unit of service provided decreases as consumption of services increases. However, while there are exceptions, ICASS and customer agencies generally have insufficient data to perform a meaningful cost analysis to quantify the potential cost savings of consolidating services to individual agencies or the government as a whole. Aside from realizing some economies of scale, State has made limited progress in lowering costs through the reengineering of ICASS administrative operations. Also, we observed that USAID may be better equipped than State to provide ICASS services to other agencies cost-effectively at some posts, but State has retained its role as service provider in almost all cases.

Nonparticipation in ICASS Services Indicates Potential Duplication

In 2004, we reported that, since the establishment of ICASS, many agencies had not signed up for ICASS services and decided instead to provide similar services for their own staff independently.[9] Providing services outside of ICASS resulted in duplicative administrative systems that limited ICASS's ability to achieve economies of scale and deliver administrative services efficiently. Our analysis of ICASS data from 2005 to 2011 shows that U.S. government agencies still do not fully participate in ICASS and are thus providing potentially duplicative administrative services for staff and operations overseas. In 2011, when agencies had a choice to obtain administrative services through ICASS, they did so 64 percent of the time, on average.[10] Participation rates for individual services ranged from nearly 22 percent to about 96 percent in 2011 (see table 1). In addition, participation rates for many services have remained relatively constant since 2005. Participation rates for 10 services have increased by 5 percentage points or less, while only 3 services have seen participation rates increase by 10 percentage points or more. An additional 12 services experienced a decrease in participation rates between 2005 and 2011. Furthermore, the ICASS participation rate was below 50 percent for eight ICASS services in 2011.

---

[9]GAO-04-511.

[10]In order to calculate the participation rate of different ICASS services, we counted the agencies at each post where the service is provided and then the number of agencies which subscribe to the service. The ratio between the two numbers is the participation rate. See appendix I for a detailed discussion of our methodology. We excluded two services, basic package and community liaison office services, which are mandatory for all agencies with U.S. direct hire, certain authorized third country nationals, U.S. contractors, and other staff at a post.

Table 1: Average Participation Rates by ICASS Service, 2005 and 2011

Service (in ascending order of 2011 participation rate)	Participation rate		Percent change between 2005 and 2011
	2005	2011	
Government-owned/long-term lease residential building operations	22.8%	21.7%	-1.1%
Budgeting and financial plans	26.1	25.0	-1.1
Vehicle maintenance	27.2	25.7	-1.5
Reproduction services	28.1	28.0	-0.1
Short-term lease nonresidential building operations	40.0	32.2	-7.8
Human resources: U.S. citizen services	46.4	35.6	-10.8
Accounts and records	43.5	39.9	-3.6
Motor pool services	37.5	45.1	7.6
Pouching services	49.2	50.2	1.0
Administrative supply	61.0	56.5	-4.6
Furniture, furnishings, and appliance pools	43.7	57.5	13.8
Short-term lease residential building operations	57.7	63.4	5.7
Payroll	63.2	65.2	2.0
Shipping and customs	67.6	66.2	-1.4
Leasing services	62.5	67.9	5.4
Government-owned/long-term lease nonresidential building operations	61.1	68.0	6.9
Nonexpendable property management	52.8	70.6	17.8
Human resources: locally employed staff	67.1	70.6	3.5
Travel services	69.1	70.7	1.5
Reception, switchboard, and telephone services	70.6	71.3	0.6
Nonresidential local guard program services	67.1	72.2	5.2
Procurement services	70.3	75.4	5.1
Information management technical support	60.9	77.6	16.7
Cashiering	80.3	81.4	1.1
Health services	80.9	83.4	2.5
Human resources services[b]	86.2	85.4	-0.8
Mail and messenger services	87.7	87.0	-0.7
Vouchering	88.0	87.6	-0.4
Information management services[b]	92.1	92.8	0.7
Security services	89.9	93.1	3.2
Financial management services[b]	91.5	94.0	2.5
General services[b]	91.1	96.2	5.1

Source: GAO analysis of ICASS data.

In some instances, nonparticipation may indicate that a service is not offered to all agencies at a post or that an agency does not need a particular service. For example, some agencies do not participate in government-owned/long-term lease residential building operations because they house their staff only in residences with short-term leases. In such instances, nonparticipation does not necessarily indicate duplication of services.

Although ICASS participation rates vary widely by agency, with the exception of USAID, individual agency rates have remained relatively constant since 2005.[11] Of the 46 non-State agencies that were present at 10 or more posts in both 2005 and 2011, 17 experienced increases in participation rates of 5 percentage points or less, while 13 saw participation increase by 10 or more points.[12] An additional 11 agencies reduced their participation in ICASS during this period. USAID has experienced a marked increase in participation since it began consolidating its administrative operations with State, from 51 percent in 2005 to 68 percent in 2011 (see app. III for detailed discussion of USAID

---

[11] In order to calculate participation rate by agencies, we counted the total number of services a particular agency participates in and the total number of services provided at the posts where that agency has a presence. The ratio of the two numbers is the participation rate by agency. See appendix I for detailed discussion of the methodology.

[12] Individual agencies may have multiple sub-agency codes for ICASS billing purposes, and participation rates generally vary by subagency code, even within the same agency. In some cases, these subagency codes correspond to a discrete unit within an agency, such as the Defense Intelligence Agency. In others, the codes correspond to accounting entities, such as USAID's Operating Expenses account. In 2011, there were 320 such subagency codes in ICASS. DOD had the most codes (152) while the other agencies within the scope of our review had between 9 and 56 codes. As a result, it is not feasible or meaningful to calculate an overall agencywide participation rate, and the figures we present here are at the subagency code level.

GAO-12-317 Embassy Management

and State consolidation).[13] However, other agencies have not significantly increased their rates of participation over this period. Table 2 shows ICASS participation rates in 2005 and 2011 for selected components of the agencies within the scope of our review with a large overseas presence.[14]

Table 2: Rate of Participation in Available Voluntary Services, by Selected Subagency Code, 2005 and 2011

Agency name (in ascending order of 2011 participation rate)	Participation rate		Percent change between 2005 and 2011
	2005	2011	
HHS, Centers for Disease Control and Prevention	54%	66%	12%
USDA, Foreign Agriculture Service	66	64	-2
Justice, Federal Bureau of Investigation/Legal Attaché	65	67	2
USAID (Operating Expenses)	51	68	17
Commerce, Foreign Commercial Service	68	71	3
DHS, Immigration and Customs Enforcement	65	70	5
DOD, Defense Intelligence Agency	82	81	-1

Source: GAO analysis of State data.

Note: This table shows one subagency code for each of the non-State agencies within the scope of our review. We chose to include the one code from each agency that was present at the most number of posts.

To the extent that agencies do not participate in ICASS services and provide these services themselves, they are creating potentially duplicative administrative systems that may not be cost effective for the U.S. government as a whole. We observed such potential duplication during our visits to four overseas missions. For example, at each post we visited, we found that instead of participating in the ICASS-managed motor pool, several agencies operated or maintained their vehicles independently. Even some units within State do not fully participate in ICASS motor pool services; for example, State's Bureau of International Narcotics and Law Enforcement participated in the ICASS motor pool in about 37 percent of

---

[13]These figures reflect USAID's largest ICASS subagency code: Operating Expenses. Other USAID codes have also seen an increase in ICASS participation since 2005, including USAID's Development Assistance code, whose participation rate increased from 37 percent to 56 percent between 2005 and 2011.

[14]USDA, Commerce, DOD, HHS, DHS, Justice, and USAID. See appendix IV for participation rates for all agency components with a presence at 10 or more posts in 2011.

the posts where it was present in 2011. In addition, many agencies procured their own appliances or shipped their own furniture, declining to participate in ICASS furniture and appliance pools, where ICASS staff would manage these pools collectively. In Manila, the financial management officer noted that agencies' opting out of these pools not only reduced the opportunity to lower the U.S. government's overall procurement costs through larger bulk ICASS purchases, it also entailed other hidden costs, including increased labor and wear and tear on property. According to this officer, over a 6-month period in 2010, ICASS service providers had to remove and reinstall furniture at embassy-managed residences 67 times as a result of agency officials being replaced in a home by officials from a different agency. Such additional work would not have been necessary if all agencies participated in one furniture and appliance pool. Additionally, in Nairobi, where virtually all agencies were colocated at the U.S. embassy compound, we observed separate, similarly equipped photocopy rooms—one for USAID staff and one for other ICASS customers—located on the same hallway.

Rationale for Agency Decisions to Opt Out of ICASS Are Not Well-Documented, though Cost and Quality Concerns Are Key Factors

While agencies may have valid justifications for not participating in ICASS services, they generally do not document their rationales or formally share them with ICASS service providers or other customer agencies. In 2004, we recommended that the ICASS Executive Board encourage agencies not participating in ICASS services to submit detailed explanations—or business cases—of how they would fulfill these service needs and at what cost. However, ICASS officials told us that ICASS Executive Board representatives from customer agencies lack the incentive to direct their agencies to participate in ICASS services or justify their decisions not to participate. Further, neither State nor ICASS systematically requests such analyses or documents the reasons why agencies choose not to participate in an ICASS service.

Agencies Cite Cost as a Reason Not to Participate in ICASS

Agencies decide to opt out of ICASS services based on a variety of factors. In response to our survey, agency representatives cited cost most frequently as a factor in their decision not to participate in ICASS.[15] Some

---

[15] Of the 269 cases where agency representatives indicated that their agency did not subscribe to a given service, the cost to the respondent's agency was cited 44 times and the quality of the service provided was cited 34 times. In 25 instances, respondents indicated that their agency's mission requirements could not be met within ICASS. Respondents cited other factors less frequently, such as headquarters guidance about participating in ICASS.

agency representatives who obtain a specific service outside of ICASS indicated that they thought that doing so was less expensive than obtaining this service through ICASS. For example, 34 of 68 representatives whose agency did not participate in the ICASS furniture and appliance pool at their post indicated that they thought obtaining this service through ICASS was more expensive than obtaining it outside of ICASS; 21 of 44 representatives said the same about motor pool services. However, in nearly half of the total responses to this question, respondents indicated that they had no basis to judge the relative costs of ICASS and non-ICASS services or did not respond to our question on this issue (see table 3).[16]

Table 3: Number of Respondents Indicating That They Think the Cost of Obtaining Services Within ICASS is More Expensive, About the Same, or Less Expensive Than Obtain Services Outside of ICASS

Service	ICASS services are more expensive	Cost of ICASS services is about the same	ICASS services are less expensive	No basis to judge or no response	Total number of responses
Furniture, furnishings, and appliance pools	34	4	5	25	68
Motor pool services	21	5	1	17	44
Shipment and customs	0	0	0	3	3
Government-owned/long-term lease residential building operations	1	1	0	8	10
Vouchering services	7	0	3	10	20
Leasing services	3	0	0	11	14
Information management technical support	10	0	2	4	16
Procurement services	5	0	3	5	13
Human resources: locally employed staff	3	0	1	12	16
Total	**84**	**10**	**15**	**95**	**204**

Source: GAO.

Separately, we asked survey respondents whether their agency had compared the cost of obtaining services within ICASS to the costs of services outside of ICASS. Responses to this question show that some

---

[16]Although respondents indicated that their agency did not participate in an ICASS service a total 269 times, the number of responses to specific follow-up questions varied, as some respondents did not choose to answer all questions.

agencies have chosen to obtain services outside of ICASS without conducting any cost analysis. Respondents indicated that their agency had compared ICASS and non-ICASS costs of services in only 62 of 205 cases where the agency did not participate in ICASS services (see table 4).

Table 4: Number of Respondents Indicating That Their Agency Obtains Services Outside of ICASS and Has or Has Not Compared the Cost of Services within and outside of ICASS

Service	Agency has compared ICASS and non-ICASS costs	Agency has *not* compared ICASS and non-ICASS costs	Don't know or no response	Total number of responses
Furniture, furnishings, and appliance pools	31	4	33	68
Motor pool services	17	8	20	45
Shipment and customs	0	0	3	3
Government-owned/long-term lease residential building operations	1	0	9	10
Vouchering services	3	8	9	20
Leasing services	1	1	12	14
Information management technical support	5	5	6	16
Procurement services	3	5	5	13
Human resources: locally employed staff	1	4	11	16
Total	**62**	**35**	**108**	**205**

Source: GAO.

Even in cases where respondents cited cost as a significant factor in their agency's decision not to participate in ICASS, respondents indicated that their agency had frequently not compared the costs of ICASS and non-ICASS services. In 41 such cases, respondents indicated that their agency had compared costs in 24 cases.

In some cases, agency officials indicated that they were able to obtain some services from their headquarters more efficiently or effectively than through ICASS. For example, a Foreign Agricultural Service (FAS) official told us that FAS had begun to obtain certain financial services from the USDA Minneapolis Finance Center rather than from ICASS providers at individual posts, since USDA is part of the National Finance Center and already provides these services to several other agencies (including GAO). FAS has estimated that shifting this workload out of ICASS has saved FAS more than $500,000 per year. Also, Commerce, DOD, and DHS officials indicated that they generally do not participate in ICASS human resource services for American staff because their staff in

Washington, D.C., are more familiar with agency personnel policies than ICASS service providers overseas and thus can provide more efficient service to their respective officials. Additionally, according to a Customs and Border Protection official in Washington, D.C., the agency is a strong advocate for centralizing some services at the Customs and Border Protection headquarters in Washington, D.C., because its administrative staff are better positioned than ICASS service providers at post to provide agency-specific services such as information technology, human resources, and budgeting.

Agency officials also told us that in some cases they would be unable to fulfill their agency's mission if they relied on ICASS services. Several officials cited their unique transportation needs in explaining their decision not to participate in the ICASS motor pool. For example, in Manila, DHS officials said they needed to maintain their own vehicles to have immediate, 24 hours-a-day access for them to conduct investigations. Several USAID and USDA officials also noted that their missions require them to take extended trips to the field that the ICASS motor pool is sometimes not able to accommodate. Our survey found that 11 of 56 respondents who indicated that they did not participate in ICASS motor pool services said that their agencies' mission requirements for motor pool could not be met within ICASS.

Consolidation of Services Leads to Cost Savings from Economies of Scale, but Quantifying These Savings Is Difficult

Our analysis of ICASS costs and observations overseas, along with State and USAID attempts to quantify the effects of consolidation, demonstrate that consolidating administrative services has led to cost savings for the U.S. government. However, because of the limited amount of cost data available, quantifying the cost savings due to consolidation has been difficult.

Economies of Scale within ICASS

State and others have maintained that greater participation in ICASS reduces the U.S. government's overall cost of posting staff overseas, due to economies of scale. In 2010, a joint State-USAID review of support services overseas found that consolidation of these services had resulted in economies of scale at 20 posts. In 2011, when many posts were considering establishing furniture pools, the ICASS Service Center noted that when agencies do not participate in these pools, efficiencies of scale are not achieved and service providers' workload increases due to separate warehousing, inventory, and ordering for different agencies. Commenting on our 2004 report, State noted that the option for customer agencies to withdraw from ICASS services has limited ICASS's ability to realize the potential benefits of economies of scale.

Our analysis of ICASS cost and workload data confirms that State and other agencies participating in ICASS have realized savings through economies of scale. As ICASS workloads increased—for example, through increased participation in ICASS services or growth in staff posted overseas—costs per unit of output have generally decreased even as total ICASS costs have increased over the last ten years. We analyzed workload data from 2000 through 2011 for 28 services within ICASS.[17] In all 28 cases, we found that costs per unit decreased, on average, as workload increased, suggesting that as more agencies participate in ICASS services and the amount of services received through ICASS increases, service provision becomes more efficient. Overall, for every 10 percent increase in ICASS workloads, unit costs decrease by 5 percent on average (see table 5). For example, if a post offers reproduction services through ICASS and one agency provides this service for itself, this agency incurs its own personnel, material, and rent costs outside of ICASS. If that agency then decides to join ICASS, it starts to share personnel and rent costs. Hypothetically, if the workload for ICASS reproduction services increases by 10 percent, our analysis suggests that the cost per copy for ICASS customers would decrease by about 6 percent, resulting in cost savings to all existing ICASS customers. Unless non-ICASS costs of reproduction services to the agency that had previously self-provided this service were significantly lower than costs to existing ICASS customers, this agency's decision to join ICASS would likely result in overall cost savings to the U.S. government.

[17]We analyzed data for all ICASS standard services, excluding the two generally mandatory services—basic package and community liaison office services—and miscellaneous services, for which workload is not well defined. See appendix I for a detailed discussion of our methodology.

Table 5: Estimated Change in ICASS Unit Costs with 10 Percent Increase in Workload

Service	Percent change in per unit cost of service
Budgeting and financial plans	**-9.2**
Nonexpendable property management	-9.1
Furniture, furnishings, and appliance pools	-8.4
Pouch services	-7.0
Travel services	-6.2
Reproduction services	-6.2
Shipment and customs	-6.1
Administrative supply	-5.6
Procurement services	-5.6
Motor pool services	-4.8
Nonresidential local guard program services	-4.7
Accounts and records	-4.4
Payroll	-4.2
Short-term lease residential building operations	-4.1
Government-owned/long-term lease nonresidential building operations	-3.8
Cashiering	-3.2
Vouchering	-3.2
Security services	-3.4
Information management technical support	-3.0
Leasing services	-3.0
Human resources: locally employed staff	-2.9
Government-owned/long-term lease residential building operations	-2.6
Human resources: U.S. citizen services	-2.3
Mail and messenger services	-1.5
Health services	-1.5
Vehicle maintenance	-1.3
Reception, switchboard, and telephone services	-1.2
Short-term lease nonresidential building operations	-0.7
Average of all services	-5.1

Source: GAO analysis of ICASS data.

| Examples of Consolidation at Specific Posts | Individual posts have reported numerous efforts to consolidate administrative operations that resulted in efficiencies. The following are examples of some of these efforts. |

- *Kenya*. During our fieldwork in Nairobi, we visited State and USAID's combined warehouses, which were consolidated in 2009. Prior to consolidation, State managed 12 units of the warehouse compound and USAID managed 6, and each agency had its own manager and inventory system, according to the embassy's general services officer. Now, all 18 units are managed under ICASS, and the former USAID warehouse manager is the ICASS manager's deputy. As a result of consolidation, this official said the embassy has reduced the number of local staff at the warehouse from 66 to approximately 50, and there is more space in the warehouse compound. Overall, according to the management counselor, the embassy has reduced the number of U.S. direct hire employees by 2 and local staff by 22 as a result of consolidation. Embassy Nairobi's Mission Strategic Plan for fiscal year 2010 noted that these efforts have resulted in an overseas administrative platform that is leaner, more flexible, and more responsive to the needs of both agencies as well as to the needs of all ICASS customers.

- *Germany*. In 2011, State's Inspector General reported that the Berlin and Frankfurt financial management offices were finalizing their consolidation into a single operation, centralized at the embassy. Under this restructuring, the Frankfurt financial office would reduce its number of local staff from 18 to 6, while Berlin would increase its staffing by 3. According to the Inspector General, the mission expects these efforts to save an estimated $700,000 annually.

- *Cambodia*. In 2006, we reported that the embassy in Phnom Penh had successfully merged four services and realized efficiency gains, and that State and USAID officials described Phnom Penh as the model project of consolidation.[18] Prior to consolidation, USAID and State motor pool drivers occupied two separate offices, but these were joined under ICASS, making better use of existing space and decreasing utility costs. Further, the consolidation of maintenance services allowed USAID in Phnom Penh to terminate its maintenance shop lease, which led to savings in utilities and rent expenses. Finally,

---

[18]GAO-06-829.

by consolidating warehouse operations, the post reported that it had realized gains in delivery times and a 40 percent decrease in the amount of space used.

Quantifying Actual Cost Savings Is Difficult Due to Limited Data on Non-ICASS Services

While our analysis shows that costs to existing ICASS customers will likely decrease as more customers join ICASS and workloads increase, we were unable to calculate the savings to the U.S. government as a whole resulting from increased participation in ICASS. Specifically, we were unable to calculate the cost implications for new agencies joining ICASS services because cost data on services outside of ICASS are generally not comparable with ICASS cost data. Moreover, as we have noted, agencies have generally not conducted such analyses.

State and USAID attempts to quantify cost savings have also been complicated by the lack of comparable data. A 2008 review of consolidation efforts to date estimated that the U.S. government had saved millions of dollars per year by reducing staff and eliminating warehouses. However, the review concluded that an exhaustive quantification of cost savings resulting from consolidation may not be possible, noting that a comprehensive study of all costs and savings would be prohibitively expensive to conduct. This review also noted that while its estimate represents a savings to the government as a whole, the impact on individual agencies would likely vary.

In 2010, the Task Force 11 report also attempted to quantify such cost savings by comparing costs before and after consolidation at 27 posts. Overall, the report found that per capita costs related to consolidation for both ICASS and USAID decreased at most posts following consolidation.[19] However, the report also determined that baseline data on non-ICASS administrative costs prior to consolidation were not available for USAID at 7 posts, which had to be excluded from the analysis. For the remaining 20 posts, the authors of the Task Force 11 report also had to make several adjustments to the preconsolidation data in order to develop comparable data sets. According to State and USAID staff who conducted this analysis, their efforts were complicated by the lack of any USAID database that tracks and segregates the costs of administrative services that USAID incurs at missions worldwide from

---

[19]In aggregate, after adjusting for several factors, the study concluded that per capita costs decreased by 1.7 percent at these posts. However, at some of these posts, per capita costs increased for a variety of reasons, which the report did not fully explain.

other operational expenses. As a result, they said, it was very difficult to compare the cost of administrative services previously provided by USAID to the cost of services provided by ICASS after consolidation.

State Has Made Limited Progress on Other Cost Containment Efforts

One of ICASS's primary goals is to contain or reduce administrative costs. Yet State, as the primary ICASS service provider, has made little progress in containing costs by reducing the need for American administrative staff overseas. Nor has State sought to maximize the cost-effectiveness of ICASS services by ensuring that the most appropriate agency deliver these services at all posts.

Innovation and Reengineering of Service Delivery Has Been Limited

In 2004, we recommended that, in addition to pursuing the elimination of duplicative administrative support structures, the ICASS Executive Board seek to contain ICASS cost by reengineering administrative processes and employing innovative managerial approaches through competitive sourcing, regionalization of services, improved technology, and adoption of other best practices developed by agencies and other posts.[20] We further noted that State had undertaken several initiatives to increase the efficiency of ICASS services, primarily by reducing the need for administrative staff overseas. However, according to ICASS management officials, State has discontinued these efforts without demonstrating significant progress in containing costs. For example, State did not fully implement a pilot effort to streamline services by requiring ICASS service providers and ICASS councils to rationalize administrative staffing levels. Moreover, State did not execute its plans to relocate some administrative support activities from overseas to the Florida Regional Center in Fort Lauderdale, which State estimated would save ICASS customers up to $140 million over 5 years. According to State and ICASS management officials, State discontinued these efforts because it determined that the potential cost savings did not outweigh the administrative burden of fully implementing them. Furthermore, they indicated that State has not undertaken any other streamlining efforts of comparable scope.

State has implemented a wide variety of smaller scale innovations that have increased efficiency of ICASS service delivery and reduced costs. These initiatives include improvements in management information collection and analysis, standardization of posts' business processes, and

---

[20]GAO-04-511.

measurement of performance and customer satisfaction. State has also realized efficiencies through reengineering and reorganization of some of its business processes. For example State established a "post support unit" to provide vouchering services to more than 90 posts worldwide from three central locations. State also implemented a program that allows staff to initiate and process procurements from alternate locations, which State indicates has been especially helpful for high danger posts, such as Iraq. Also, in 2011, State implemented a global network energy management program, which has reportedly reduced energy costs by almost $900,000 in its first 10 months. Other than this initiative, State has not identified the specific cost impacts of these innovations. State anticipates future cost savings from innovative approaches it has undertaken in procurement of air freight pouch and mail services and information technology equipment.

Officials from nearly every agency we met with expressed concern about State's failure to contain the cost of the ICASS services it provides. In particular, agency officials in Washington, D.C., and at the overseas posts we visited commonly complained that State employed too many American staff overseas to provide administrative services instead of relying on much less expensive locally employed staff or outsourcing to local firms.[21] Officials from State's Office of Management Policy, Rightsizing, and Innovation indicated that significant ICASS cost savings were elusive unless State reduces the number of management-related American staff overseas. Yet, according to State, many posts have noted that security concerns have been a barrier to having local staff perform functions normally performed by Americans, and State has acknowledged that empowering local staff remains a challenge. In contrast, USAID officials pointed to numerous instances in which locally employed USAID staff have effectively provided administrative services, such as local procurement and real property leasing. Similarly, DOD officials in Manila asserted that local repair shops could provide car maintenance services at a lower cost than the State-run ICASS shop. However, because State is generally the only ICASS service provider, the interagency ICASS Executive Board has limited power to determine the numbers of ICASS service provider staff overseas.

---

[21]In 2004, we found that the per capita labor cost of an American direct hire staff was almost eight times higher than that of a local hire.

Although State management counselors and the interagency ICASS councils at individual posts are empowered to undertake cost containment efforts, State and ICASS management officials indicated that the councils have generally failed to do so. We found that ICASS service providers at individual posts have implemented a variety of small scale efforts to contain costs, but these efforts have not resulted in significant savings. According to a DHS official responsible for managing the overseas costs of his agency, posts' cost reduction plans have been largely limited to superficial efforts, which are unlikely to provide significant savings, such as installing energy efficient light bulbs. We found that in some cases State has limited local ICASS councils' ability to undertake more significant cost-saving initiatives. Moreover, we found instances where State has reversed ICASS councils' cost containment decisions. In Nairobi, after the council had approved a modest increase in local administrative staff salaries, the ambassador overruled this decision and directly promised all local staff a significantly larger pay increase without consulting the ICASS council. Management officials in Tokyo told us that prior to the transition to a new travel system, the embassy had vouchers processed in Bangkok, where the cost of this service was much lower. However, after the implementation of the new system, voucher processing shifted back to Tokyo, increasing the cost of this service. Finally, a senior State management official told us that ICASS councils and management officers are frequently dissuaded from outsourcing administrative operations by State regional security officers, who object due to security concerns.

Restricted Use of Alternate ICASS Service Providers Limits Opportunities for Greater Efficiencies

Although State provides virtually all ICASS services, in some cases, an agency other than State may be able to provide one or more of these services through ICASS to agencies more cost effectively at a given post. In several instances of duplication we observed, USAID appeared to have more expertise in providing a particular service than the existing State ICASS provider, potentially making USAID a reasonable alternate ICASS provider. For example, in Nairobi, USAID operates a copy center for its own staff inside the embassy compound, offering more specialized services, including digitization, than the ICASS copy center provides. In addition, staff in several focus groups we convened overseas indicated that drivers in USAID motor pools traditionally have valuable communications and navigation skills that State's ICASS drivers do not always possess, making USAID drivers particularly useful for trips outside the capital city. In Kigali, the management counselor noted that USAID human resources staff had experience in a broader range of employment contracts than their State ICASS counterparts and could potentially provide its services to both agencies.

State's *Foreign Affairs Handbook* recognizes that an agency other than State may be better positioned to be the principal provider of specific services for themselves and other agencies at a given post. It allows for the use of these alternate service providers in cases where an agency has a sufficiently large administrative support capability at a location and agrees to provide services to other agencies at that post. However, in 2006, State and USAID, in the interest of simplifying and expediting the consolidation of their administrative operations overseas, adopted a policy effectively restricting the establishment of new alternate ICASS service providers. This policy applied to posts where State and USAID would colocate between fiscal years 2007 and 2010. As a result, in 2012, only seven posts had such a provider for one or more ICASS service, potentially limiting opportunities for ICASS to achieve greater efficiency and effectiveness. In 2010, Task Force 11, a joint State-USAID group supporting the development of the Quadrennial Diplomacy and Development Review,[22] recommended that posts consider the use of alternate service providers in order to reduce costs. Task Force 11 also proposed that State and USAID establish a Joint Management Board and formulate a consolidation policy that considers the use of alternate providers. However, the Joint Management Board, created in August 2011, has not yet established such a policy.

ICASS Customers Generally Satisfied, and Management Has New Tools to Monitor Quality in Some Areas

Results from the annual ICASS survey, and our own survey of U.S. government agency representatives overseas, show that survey respondents are generally satisfied with the quality of ICASS services. Furthermore, officials in focus groups we conducted at four posts generally felt that ICASS provided quality administrative services. Nonetheless, some dissatisfaction with ICASS performance still exists, especially among USAID staff, and in some cases, ICASS performance problems could affect some agencies' ability to achieve their respective missions efficiently and effectively. State has begun implementing tools that improve managers' ability to monitor and evaluate performance and customer satisfaction; however, the standards do not measure performance for some aspects of services that agencies have reported are particularly problematic.

---

[22]Department of State and the U.S. Agency for International Development, *Leading Through Civilian Power: The First Quadrennial Diplomacy and Development Review* (Washington, D.C.: Dec. 15, 2010).

Surveys of Service Recipients Show Overall Satisfaction with ICASS

Results from the annual ICASS survey, and our survey of ICASS service recipients, show that respondents are generally satisfied with overall ICASS services, although results varied for some agencies and services. While some dissatisfaction exists among some customer agencies, officials we interviewed at four posts were generally satisfied with ICASS services.

ICASS Survey Shows Overall Satisfaction

The ICASS Service Center uses its annual ICASS Customer Satisfaction Survey to gauge overall satisfaction with each administrative service provided at a post. In 2011, the ICASS Service Center reported a 67 percent response rate to the survey, with nearly 47,000 responses from 234 posts worldwide. Service recipients, which include American and local staff, dependents of American personnel overseas, and ICASS service providers, access the survey through the Internet to evaluate ICASS services they received over the past year. Although we found limitations with the methodology of this survey, customers have generally reported overall satisfaction with ICASS services since the ICASS Service Center began conducting this survey in 2005.[23] On a scale from 1 to 5, a score of 2 or lower indicates a customer's dissatisfaction with a service and a score of 4 or higher indicates satisfaction. (A score of 3 is labeled as "neutral.") The average score for overall satisfaction from all survey respondents ranged from 3.95 in 2005 to 4.03 in 2011 (see fig. 2).

---

[23]In reviewing the survey results, we found that the response rate for several posts exceeded 100 percent. ICASS officials indicated that they use human resources population-at-post data to determine the total number of eligible survey respondents when calculating the response rate. Eligible respondents are notified through flyers, newsletters, and e-mails to complete the web-based survey anonymously. Because the survey administration was anonymous, it is difficult to determine potential bias in the results. Therefore, the results may only reflect the views of the respondents and not all service recipients.

Figure 2: ICASS Customer Satisfaction Scores on a Scale from 1 to 5 for Selected Agencies, 2005 through 2011

ICASS customer satisfaction score

	All agencies[a]
- - - -	State[b]
▬ ▪ ▬ ▪	USAID
▨ ▨ ▨ ▨	Other agencies[c]

Source: ICASS Service Center.

Note: Respondents were asked to rate the extent to which they agreed or disagreed with the statement, "Overall, I am satisfied with this service," with 1 = strongly disagree; 2 = disagree; 3 = neutral; 4 = agree; 5 = strongly agree. Data for "all agencies" include responses from ICASS service providers.

[a]"All agencies" include responses from all ICASS customers.

[b]"State" includes responses from ICASS service providers, who are almost always State employees.

[c]"Other agencies" include responses from USDA, Commerce, DOD, HHS, DHS, and Justice.

Though results of the ICASS annual survey have consistently indicated that service recipients who have responded to the survey are generally satisfied, the survey data also indicate that responses from agencies other than State consistently express lower levels of overall satisfaction, as shown in figure 2. In addition, the most recent survey data show that responses to overall satisfaction with ICASS services vary by agency and service. For example, in 2011, State respondents expressed somewhat higher satisfaction with ICASS than did USAID and other agency respondents (see table 6). Also, 21 services received satisfaction scores above 4, including the 2 highest-ranked services: cashiering and information management technical support (each with a score of 4.24). Only one service—leasing—received a score below 3.85.

Table 6: Average Customer Satisfaction Scores on a Scale from 1 to 5 by Agency for 2011

Agency	Overall satisfaction score	Number of respondents
ICASS service providers[a]	4.25	13,628
State	4.00	23,424
HHS	3.94	911
Commerce	3.88	566
USDA	3.87	393
DOD	3.87	2,435
Justice	3.81	663
DHS	3.70	539
USAID	3.64	3,163

Source: ICASS Service Center.

Note: Respondents were asked to evaluate overall ICASS services by indicating whether they agreed or disagreed with the statement, "Overall, I am satisfied with this service," with 1 = strongly disagree; 2 = disagree; 3 = neutral; 4 = agree; 5 = strongly agree.

[a]The annual ICASS survey reports responses from ICASS service providers separately. In almost all cases, these service providers are State employees.

Our Survey Results Also Show Overall Satisfaction with ICASS Services Among the Largest Agencies

We surveyed ICASS Council representatives from the eight largest ICASS customer agencies regarding the quality of ICASS services.[24] Nearly 80 percent of all responses indicated that the quality of services received through ICASS was "good" or better (see fig. 3). Only about 6 percent of responses indicated that the quality was "poor".[25] For example, 133 of 152 respondents (88 percent) who receive information technology services through ICASS indicated that the quality of this service was "good" or better. Similarly, 141 of 163 respondents (87 percent) rated shipping and customs services "good" or better.

---

[24]These agencies were State, DOD, USAID, Commerce, USDA, Justice, DHS, and HHS. We also included USAID executive officers in our survey. We chose these respondents because we determined that they had sufficient knowledge to answer questions regarding the cost and quality of administrative services at their posts.

[25]In our survey, 184 respondents rated the quality of up to nine services, providing 1,292 total responses to the question regarding quality. Of the total responses for all services, 1,008 responses indicated that quality was "good" or better, while 82 responses indicated the quality was "poor."

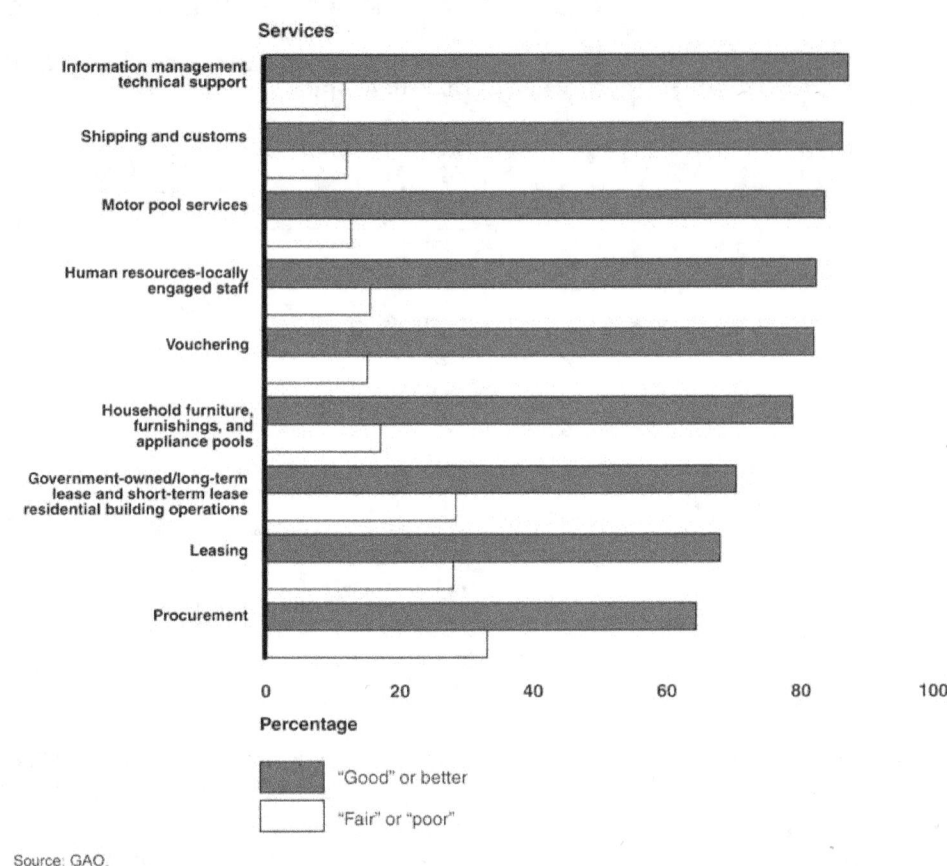

Figure 3: Customer Perceptions on the Quality of Selected ICASS Services, 2011

Source: GAO.

Note: Our survey asked respondents to rate the quality of each of the selected services in which they participated as either excellent, very good, good, fair, or poor. "Good" or better includes good, very good, and excellent responses.

While survey respondents indicated that they were generally satisfied with the nine services included in our survey, about 30 percent of responses rated their satisfaction as "fair" or "poor" for three of the nine services. For example, 42 of 150 respondents (28 percent) who receive leasing services through ICASS indicated that the quality of this service was "fair" or "poor." Similarly, 52 of 157 (33 percent) rated procurement "fair" or "poor."

Agency Officials We Interviewed at Four Posts Were Generally Satisfied with ICASS Services

At the four posts we visited, ICASS customers were generally satisfied with the services they received. Participants in our focus groups were particularly satisfied with reception and telephone services, medical services, security services, and human resources services for local staff. For example, officials in Tokyo said the embassy's telephone operators were very helpful, especially for staff who spoke little or no Japanese. State and USAID officials in Nairobi also found the embassy's medical services helpful and noted that although customers must now schedule appointments ahead of time, medical unit staff can normally see the patient on the day of the request. On the other hand, some staff at posts we visited registered complaints about other services, including household maintenance and motor pool. However, senior USAID officials we interviewed noted that, despite some staff complaints, there had been few reductions in services that negatively impacted USAID officials' ability to complete their mission at post.

Some Dissatisfaction with Administrative Services Persists

Despite the general levels of satisfaction expressed in our survey and in the annual ICASS Customer Satisfaction Survey, some dissatisfaction still exists, potentially limiting agencies' participation in ICASS. Furthermore, in some cases, agency officials indicated that poor delivery of administrative service could impact the ability of agencies to achieve their missions overseas efficiently and effectively. In particular, we found that USAID personnel have concerns about the ability of ICASS to meet their unique requirements; some ICASS customers perceive that their agencies' service requests receive lower priority than other agencies' requests; and common errors in ICASS billing create inefficiencies and additional administrative burdens for customer agencies, according to some of the agency officials we interviewed.

USAID Concerns

USAID respondents have consistently rated ICASS services lower than other agencies in the annual ICASS survey. Some USAID staff we interviewed overseas expressed a concern that they have lost or would lose control over their administrative operations after consolidating with State, resulting in a lower level of responsiveness from administrative service providers than they were accustomed to. In addition, in 2010, the American Foreign Service Association (AFSA) conducted a survey to document the views of USAID officials about the ongoing consolidation of State and USAID administrative operations. According to AFSA, the results of this survey highlighted concerns about the morale of USAID staff overseas. Although we found that this survey has several limitations,[26] it highlights serious concerns that some USAID staff had about consolidating some support services. In particular, according to a 2010 AFSA report on the results of this survey, USAID personnel have serious complaints about the quality of motor pool services, property maintenance, information technology, and the treatment and compensation of locally employed staff. In addition, research conducted by a joint State and USAID task force in 2010 found that consolidation had had a negative impact on 20 percent of USAID respondents and 3 percent of State respondents surveyed.[27]

Equitable Treatment in Service Priority and Quality

In 2004, we reported that some ICASS customers expressed the opinion that service provision was not always equitable and that State employees received preferential treatment in both the quality and priority of services provided; however, we further reported that we could find no evidence of systematic preferential treatment to support such claims. In our 2011 survey, the majority of non-State respondents indicated that their agency's requests were given the same priority as State's requests for six of the nine services included in the questionnaire (see table 7). However, at least one-third of respondents thought that their agency's requests received lower priority than State requests for five of the nine services. In addition, some respondents in our survey commented that ICASS service allocated better quality furniture to State than to other agencies.

---

[26]AFSA officials administered an anonymous Web-based survey to overseas USAID Foreign Service officers, U.S. personal service contractors, and Foreign Service nationals from March 15, 2010, to April 2, 2010, and received 1,073 responses. Because the survey administration was anonymous, it is difficult to determine any potential bias in the results. Therefore, the survey results may only reflect the views of the respondents and not those of all USAID personnel. In addition, questions in the survey may have biased the respondent to answer in a manner favorable to the organization conducting the survey.

[27]Department of State and the U.S. Agency for International Development, *Leading Through Civilian Power: The First Quadrennial Diplomacy and Development Review* (Washington, D.C.: Dec. 15, 2010), p. 203.

GAO-12-317 Embassy Management

Table 7: Responses from USAID and Other Agency Personnel as to Whether They Receive Higher or Lower Priority than State Personnel When Requesting ICASS Services.

Service	Number of respondents indicating higher priority	Number of respondents indicating about the same	Number of respondents indicating lower priority	No basis to judge or no response	Total responses
Furniture pool	0	32	20	7	59
Motor pool	2	33	28	8	71
Shipping and customs	0	82	23	12	117
Government-owned/long-term lease and short-term lease residential building operations	2	54	47	8	111
Vouchering services	0	68	18	12	98
Leasing services	2	47	37	15	101
Information management technical support services	2	60	27	12	101
Procurement services	1	55	39	14	109
Human resources: locally employed staff services	1	70	22	12	105

Source: GAO survey.

Note: Our survey asked respondents to indicate whether their agency's requests for ICASS services were given a higher or lower priority than State requests as much higher, somewhat higher, about the same, somewhat lower, or much lower than State.

AFSA's report on the results of its 2010 survey indicate that "USAID employees feel ignored and upset at the treatment they have received from their State counterparts." In particular, according to this report, when ICASS providers take over building, warehouse, and residence operations, USAID staff experience poorer maintenance service and smaller working spaces compared to State personnel.

Despite such perceptions, we found no concrete evidence that State received preferential treatment from ICASS service providers. In Nairobi, for example, the management officer said that USAID staff often complained that they had less access to the ICASS motor pool than State officials and therefore had to frequently travel to meetings by taxi. However, in response to comments in the annual survey, the management section analyzed the post's taxi usage from 2007 through 2010 and found that the perception that the motor pool assigned taxis to USAID staff more than to other embassy staff was incorrect.

Billing Errors	Officials from several agencies we spoke with said that their annual ICASS invoices often contain numerous errors, which require a significant amount of effort to correct. For example, USDA conducted an analysis of its ICASS workload counts for fiscal year 2011 and found that 22 of the 100 cases it reviewed contained discrepancies that required corrections. At one post we visited, the DOD ICASS Council representative said he and his staff were able to reduce DOD's share of the post's total ICASS expenses from 9.6 to 6.5 percent by identifying and correcting errors, such as being charged for space that they did not occupy. Commerce officials said they had identified an instance in which the ICASS service provider did not cancel a lease for an unoccupied building for many months, resulting in higher than necessary ICASS costs for all customer agencies at the post. In its 2010 report on ICASS, AFSA reported that USAID staff spend "an enormous amount of time in checking of vouchers and services due to an increase in inappropriate billings and mistakes." Further, a DHS official said that a component agency identified an error in its ICASS bill at one post that had caused a 50 percent increase in its security charges. This official noted, however, that while identifying and correcting such errors saves his department money, it does not save money for the government as a whole because correcting the error merely redistributes the costs being shared by all the agencies served by ICASS at the post in question.

New Management Tools Measure Some Aspects of Quality of ICASS Services

State has implemented management tools to identify and address performance and satisfaction issues in a timelier manner. In 2007, State launched the Collaborative Management Initiative, a process that included input from service providers in the field to draft standards and performance metrics for ICASS services that would apply to all posts. Prior to this initiative, service standards were inconsistent and varied by post. This effort resulted in the creation and implementation of uniform service standards and eServices—an online software program to request services and give service providers immediate feedback on the quality of each service rendered. In addition, the eServices program captures and reports to management performance-related metrics on the volume of services provided, and the extent to which service providers are meeting performance standards. However, these metrics do not address some concerns about service quality raised to us by customer agencies.

Uniform Service Standards

In 2008, State developed about 50 uniform service standards to provide consistent requirements among posts for fulfilling administrative service requests—such as the time required to complete a residential repair or provide transportation to a meeting. State began measuring each post's performance against these standards in 2010. A 2008 review of State-USAID consolidation to date stated that implementing these service standards would allow analysis of the most cost-effective means to provide administrative support services at the maximum possible quality levels.[28] State officials commented that the implementation of these standards has focused attention on service delivery at posts and, as a result, improved service delivery.

In fiscal year 2011, 64 percent of all ICASS services for which standards had been set met their specific service standard. According to State data, ICASS service providers received more than 1.5 million requests for these services worldwide in fiscal year 2011, more than 1 million of which were completed within the specified standard.[29] For example, post motor pools logged more than 600,000 requests for local trips in fiscal year 2011, and ICASS service providers were able to fulfill nearly 74 percent of these requests within 4 hours. In addition, post motor pools logged more than 6,100 requests for nonlocal trips in fiscal year 2011, and ICASS service providers were able to fulfill about 69 percent of these requests within 5 business days. Table 8 lists selected services and their uniform service standard along with fiscal year 2011 performance data.

---

[28] Joint Management Council, *Consolidation After-Action Review: Best Practices and Lessons Learned from Tier 1 Posts* (Washington, D.C.: Nov. 2008).

[29] Figures represent requests for the 49 services that State currently tracks through the Uniform Service Standards. Because State has identified more than 200 unique services that are provided through ICASS, these figures are a fraction of the total number of requests that ICASS service providers received in fiscal year 2011.

Table 8: Selected ICASS Services and Uniform Service Standards with the Percentage of Service Completions Meeting Standards, Fiscal Year 2011

Service category	Specific Service	Uniform service standard	Number of services completed	Percentage of service completions meeting standard
Motor pool services	Local transportation by car-and-driver (government-owned or contract) or other cost-effective alternatives such as self-drives or taxis	Submit request for a vehicle 4 business hours in advance for local trips.	631,473	73.8%
Motor pool services	Non-local trips	Submit request for a vehicle 5 business days in advance for nonlocal trips.	6,135	68.7%
Travel services	Make transportation and hotel reservations	Make, change, or cancel transportation or hotel reservations and inform customer within 1 business day.	37,152	66.2
Reception and switchboard services	Issue visitor passes	Visitor passes issued within 15 minutes of arrival.	22,695	60.0
Information management technical support services	Minor trouble shooting, maintenance, and routine tasks performed by the Information Technology staff	Respond to routine Help Desk support requests within 4 business hours and achieve a customer satisfaction level of 95% or better.	181,075	58.6
Residential building operations services	Minor repair and maintenance	Routine minor repairs and maintenance completed in 7 business days.	71,479	58.6

Source: State.

Note: Uniform service standards in this table are only a sample of the 195 service standards.

eServices Customer Feedback Results

At the end of fiscal year 2010, 83 percent of overseas posts were using the service request software program, eServices, to generate customer feedback in order to improve support services. State began tracking customer feedback results in fiscal year 2010, and the scores have generally increased from fiscal year 2010 to 2011. The eServices feedback survey uses a scale of 1 to 5, with a score of 2 or lower indicating dissatisfaction and a score of 3 or higher indicating some level of satisfaction. For fiscal year 2011, 14 services received an average score of 4 or higher, compared to 7 services in fiscal year 2010 (see table 9).

GAO-12-317 Embassy Management

Table 9: eServices Point-of-Service Ratings, on a Scale from 1 to 5, by Service, Fiscal Years 2010 and 2011

Service (in descending order of 2011 survey rating)	Average survey rating	
	2010	2011
Community Liaison Office Services	4.12	4.38
Information management technical services	4.04	4.24
Payrolling services	4.32	4.24
Shipping and customs	3.96	4.24
Nonexpendable property management	3.96	4.19
Travel services	4.00	4.18
Human resources: locally employed staff	3.99	4.16
Vouchering services	3.83	4.16
Motor pool services	3.88	4.15
Human resources: U.S. citizen services	4.18	4.12
Long-term lease nonresidential building operations	3.84	4.12
Basic package	4.04	4.09
Reception, switchboard, and telephone services	3.94	4.09
Health services	4.27	4.07
Administrative supply	3.74	3.99
Security services	3.66	3.91
Procurement services	3.70	3.90
Long-term lease residential building operations	3.70	3.87
Leasing services	3.89	3.82

Source: State.

Note: Respondents were asked to rate the level of their level of satisfaction with their last eServices transaction: 1 = very dissatisfied; 2 = dissatisfied; 3 = somewhat satisfied; 4 = satisfied; 5 = very satisfied.

Performance Metrics Do Not Address Some Aspects of ICASS Customer Dissatisfaction

The metrics that State is using to measure performance against standards do not address some concerns about service quality raised to us by customer agencies. Moreover, since State's performance reporting to the missions does not disaggregate results by customer agency, it does not reflect the extent to which service delivery is equitable across agencies. Nor do State's metrics gauge progress on reducing the incidents of ICASS billing errors.

In November 2011, we reported that obtaining customer input to meet customer needs is a key operating principle for effective management of cost-sharing systems, such as ICASS, used to conduct business-like activities within and between federal agencies.[30] State's process for establishing uniform service standards is informed by input from ICASS service providers and customer agency officials in Washington, D.C. However, it is not clear that these standards address common concerns of overseas ICASS customers. A State management counselor we spoke to in Nairobi indicated that achieving the uniform service standards does not necessarily constitute acceptable performance for many of their customers. This opinion was echoed by customer agency representatives in focus groups and interviews we conducted overseas. For example, USAID officials have cited the unavailability of ICASS motor pool vehicles for travel to distant project sites as a major impediment to achieving their mission. Although ICASS performance standards call for the motor pool to provide nonlocal transportation within 5 business days of receiving a request, USAID officials indicated that they often need vehicles more quickly than this to effectively monitor their projects.

In responding to a draft of this report, both State and USAID indicated that more meaningful customer input is needed to establish appropriate performance standards and address areas of dissatisfaction. According to USAID, the process for developing the current standards resulted in the preeminence of service provider views over those of customers. State indicated that it needs greater input from customer agencies at posts about the services that they consider problematic so that concerns can be addressed. State also indicated that it is planning to implement new systems to capture more customer feedback and other performance data that will enable the department to recalibrate existing service standards and develop new ones.

Conclusions

In the current budget environment, the obligation of agencies to review their operations to identify areas of duplication and overlap and to

---

[30]GAO, *Intragovernmental Revolving Funds: Commerce Departmental and Census Working Capital Funds Should Better Reflect Key Operating Principles*, GAO-12-56 (Washington, D.C: Nov. 18, 2011). This report discusses key principles for effective management of Intragovernmental Revolving Funds, such as Working Capital Funds. The ICASS Working Capital Fund is a no-year fund that permits posts to retain a portion of their unobligated funds from one fiscal year to the next.

consider areas for potential cost savings has become critically important. In 2004, we recommended that the ICASS Executive Board pursue the elimination of duplicative administrative support structures with the goal of limiting each service to one provider at U.S. facilities overseas. While State and USAID have made notable progress in consolidating their administrative operations, overall participation in ICASS has not increased significantly, and agencies are likely missing opportunities to take advantage of clear economies of scale. The voluntary nature of ICASS has permitted the continuation of duplicative services, as agencies often make decisions about participating in ICASS based on their own costs and not the costs to the U.S. government as a whole. While agencies may opt out of ICASS because they believe they can obtain less costly services on their own, doing so may actually increase the overall cost to the U.S. government. Since agencies usually do not formally justify their decisions to opt out of ICASS or routinely conduct cost analyses, in some cases their decisions may be based more on poorly supported perceptions of cost and quality than on hard data and facts. Because ICASS management lacks comparable data on the cost of overseas administrative services within and outside of ICASS, it is poorly positioned to convince agencies that greater participation in ICASS services is in their own interest or that of the U.S. government overall. Moreover, ICASS has still not led to systematic innovation and reengineering of administrative services delivery, especially those which would reduce the need for expensive American staff overseas and thus reduce costs significantly and make participation in ICASS more cost-effective for agencies. State and USAID may also be missing opportunities for achieving greater efficiency and effectiveness by limiting the use of USAID, in lieu of State, as an alternate ICASS service provider. We have previously recommended that the ICASS Executive Board encourage greater ICASS participation and pursue other streamlining efforts. However, experience has shown that board members do not necessarily have the incentive to require their agencies to participate in ICASS, especially if they are unconvinced that it is in their agency's financial self-interest. The board has also had limited power to effectuate reengineering and innovation in administrative processes, as State maintains control over virtually all of these processes as both the primary provider and customer of ICASS services. In this context, congressional action may be necessary to increase participation in ICASS. Finally, without more comprehensive performance data, ICASS service providers are poorly positioned to demonstrate to the agencies that they are focusing on critical areas of dissatisfaction with ICASS that could be impediments to achieving agency missions.

Matter for Congressional Consideration

In order to contain costs and reduce duplication of administrative support services overseas, Congress may wish to consider requiring agencies to participate in ICASS services unless they provide a business case to show that they can obtain these services outside of ICASS without increasing overall costs to the U.S. government or that their mission cannot be achieved within ICASS.

Recommendation for Executive Action

The Secretary of State should increase the cost effectiveness of ICASS services by continuing to reengineer administrative processes and seek innovative managerial approaches, including those that would reduce the reliance on American officials overseas to provide these services.

Where agencies are able to demonstrate, through a compelling business case, that they can provide a service more efficiently than the existing State ICASS provider without adverse effects on the overall government budget, we recommend that the Secretary of State and the Administrator of USAID allow the creation of new ICASS service providers, in lieu of State, that could provide administrative services to the other agencies at individual posts.

To help ensure that ICASS provides satisfactory and equitable administrative service, we also recommend that the Secretary of State, in close coordination with ICASS customer agencies, develop additional uniform service standards and other performance measures that gauge ICASS service providers' progress in resolving major sources of customer dissatisfaction.

Agency Comments and Our Evaluation

We provided a draft of this report to the agencies within the scope of our review for their comment. State, USAID, USDA, Commerce, and DHS provided written comments which are reproduced in appendices V through IX along with our responses to specific points. DOD, HHS, and DOJ did not provide written comments. The agencies and the ICASS Service Center also provided technical comments that were incorporated, as appropriate.

State and USAID generally concurred with the report's conclusions and recommendations. However, while State agreed that continued efforts are needed to increase the cost effectiveness of ICASS services, it did not agree that such actions have not been undertaken or that such efforts would substantially reduce the need for the American management staff abroad. We added information about State's other cost reduction efforts, noting that they were of a smaller scale than those State had indicated in 2004 that it would undertake. Given the relatively high cost of posting American management staff overseas compared to engaging staff locally, we believe that even minor modifications in staffing could have significant cost implications and should be thoroughly explored, in close coordination with ICASS-participating agencies. We modified our recommendation to clarify that reengineering of administrative processes and innovative managerial approaches should include such staff reductions but not be limited to them necessarily.

USDA, Commerce, and DHS took issue with our finding that nonparticipation in ICASS services reflects potential duplication of administrative services overseas and with our suggestion that Congress consider requiring agencies to participate in ICASS services unless they provide a business case to justify opting out. In particular, these agencies noted that ICASS customers have a variety of valid reasons for not participating in ICASS services and expressed concern that developing business cases to justify nonparticipation would be overly burdensome. We believe that, while agencies may have valid reasons for not participating in some ICASS services, the voluntary nature of ICASS has permitted agencies to opt out of the system without conducting rigorous cost analyses. Without such analyses, agencies are making decisions about participating in ICASS based on their own costs—or perceptions of cost—and not necessarily the overall cost to the U.S. government. We believe that if conducted in close coordination with the ICASS Service Center and other participating agencies, preparing business cases need not be overly burdensome and could lead to significant, long term savings for the U.S. government that would justify the additional effort.

As agreed with your office, unless you publicly announce the contents of this report earlier, we plan no further distribution until 28 days from the report date. At that time, we will send copies to the appropriate congressional committees, the Secretary of State, and other interested parties. In addition, the report will be available at no charge on the GAO website at http://www.gao.gov.

Should you or your staff have questions concerning this report, please contact me at (202) 512-8980 or courtsm@gao.gov. Contact points for our Offices of Congressional Relations and Public Affairs may be found on the last page of this report. Key contributors to this report are listed in appendix X.

Michael J. Courts
Acting Director
International Affairs and Trade

Appendix I: Objectives, Scope, and Methodology

General

In response to a congressional request to update our 2004 report on the International Cooperative Administrative Support Services (ICASS) system and review ICASS's progress in improving its efficiency, we assessed (1) the extent to which changes in ICASS participation have affected the duplication and cost of administrative support services and (2) customer satisfaction with the quality of ICASS services overseas.

Our review focused on the eight agencies with the largest ICASS invoices: the Departments of Agriculture (USDA), Commerce (Commerce), Defense (DOD), Health and Human Services (HHS), Homeland Security (DHS), Justice (DOJ), and State (State), as well as the United States Agency for International Development (USAID). Together, these agencies accounted more than 98 percent of the total ICASS budget in 2010. We reviewed data on these agencies' participation in ICASS, including their costs and results of the annual ICASS Customer Satisfaction Survey, from 2005 to 2011. We interviewed officials at each agency as well as at the ICASS Service Center. We also conducted fieldwork at four overseas locations: Tokyo, Japan; Nairobi, Kenya; Manila, the Philippines; and Kigali, Rwanda. At each location, we observed administrative services, met with embassy management officials, and conducted focus groups of ICASS customers. We chose these locations based on the size of and number of agencies at the post; status of consolidation of USAID's and State's administrative platforms; cost of obtaining services in the host country; and geographic diversity.

To assess the extent to which changes in ICASS participation have affected the duplication and cost of administrative support services, we analyzed data from the ICASS Global Database, which is maintained by the ICASS Service Center and contains information for each ICASS service and subagency code at each overseas post on: workloads; billing by agency; unit costs; and other information necessary for operating the system. As described in the following section, we assessed the strength of these data and compared them against other ICASS data. We found these data sufficiently reliable for the purposes of describing customer agencies' participation rates in ICASS and demonstrating the economies of scale that occur as ICASS workloads increase.

Participation Rate

We used annual data generated through the ICASS Global Database and data prepared by the ICASS Service Center for the purposes of its annual customer satisfaction survey to analyze participation rates. The data cover ICASS services provided from 2005 to 2011 and contain information on the level of services an agency is billed for at all the posts where it has a presence. In order to compare these data across fiscal years, we corrected inconsistencies in the names of the posts and agencies before we merged the annual data. Because two ICASS services—basic service and community liaison service—are generally mandatory,[1] all agencies with an overseas presence should be covered in the ICASS Global Database, even if they choose to provide all nonmandatory services outside ICASS. To assess the reliability of these data, we interviewed knowledgeable officials regarding the collection and maintenance of these data. We also tested some of these data electronically against data prepared by the ICASS Service Center for the annual ICASS customer satisfaction survey. We determined the data were sufficiently reliable for the purposes of reporting ICASS participation rates by agency and by service.

Using these data, we analyzed participation rates for different ICASS services. Participation rate by ICASS service measures the proportion of agencies at a post that use ICASS for a particular service. A higher participation rate indicates the service has more agencies participating than a service with a lower participation rate. This analysis helps us identify how "popular" a service is: whether agencies use this service provided through ICASS or opt out and provide a similar service for themselves. In order to calculate the participation rate by ICASS service, we first counted the number of agencies which participate in a particular service at a post, and then we summed this number across all the posts where the service is provided through ICASS. Next, we calculated the total number of agencies at all the posts where the service is provided, which is also the maximum number of agencies potentially participating in a service if every agency chooses to use ICASS. The ratio between the two sums is the participation rate of a service. Our calculation may overestimate the non-participation rate if agencies do not participate in ICASS because they do not have "real needs" for certain services. However, without detailed "needs assessments" from every agency at every post, it is not possible to differentiate non-participation because of

---

[1]These two services are mandatory for all agencies at a post with U.S. direct hires and certain authorized third-country national, U.S. contractor, or other staff. Basic package—which includes several services that can only be obtained by the embassy, such as securing diplomatic credentials from the host country—and community liaison office services are generally mandatory. Participation rates are not 100 percent for these services because an agency may have only local staff at a given post, and these staff are not required to participate in these two services. In such cases, agencies may receive some services from ICASS, but not basic package or community liaison office services.

no "real needs" from non-participation due to duplication of services. We
used the ICASS standard cost center definitions in our analysis. The
standard cost centers, with 31 services, define the services in more detail
than the "lite" cost centers, which bunches some services in broader
categories and contains 16 services.

We also analyzed participation rates for different agencies. The ICASS
Global Database contains data at the subagency code level, which is the
level at which ICASS invoices are calculated. Some agencies have
numerous subagency codes—for example, DOD has more than 150 such
codes—while others have few. We calculated and presented data on
participation rates at the subagency code level. Participation rate by
agency measures the amount of ICASS services an agency uses as a
proportion of the total number of services offered through ICASS at the
posts where an agency has a presence. A higher participation rate
indicates the agency uses ICASS more than an agency with a lower
participation rate. This analysis helps us identify the range of agencies
deciding to get services through ICASS: a 100 percent participation rate
indicates that an agency uses all the ICASS services provided at each
post where it has a presence. In order to calculate the participation rate
by agency, we calculated the total number of ICASS services an agency
participates in at a post. We determined the maximum number of services
that a post offers. Next, we summed the total number of ICASS services
an agency participates in and the maximum number of services offered at
all the posts where the agency has a presence. The ratio of the two sums
is the participation rate of the agency. Because we are interested in how
agencies choose to provide the services when they have a choice, we
excluded two mandatory services from our calculation, the basic service
and community liaison service.

Economies of Scale

We reviewed economics literature to understand the factors driving
economies of scale. We also reviewed the econometric method used to
identify evidence of economies of scale and test the hypothesis of
increased production level leading to lower average cost.

To determine whether there was evidence of economies of scale within
ICASS, and the extent of these potential economies, we obtained data
generated through ICASS Global Database. These data cover ICASS
services provided from 2000 to 2010 at approximately 180 posts and
contain information on the units of services provided (known as
workload), the cost of the services, and the location of each post. See
table 10 for a summary statistics of the numeric variables in the data.

Table 10: Summary Statistics of ICASS Data

Name of variables	Units	Number of observations	Mean	Standard deviation	Minimum	Maximum
Total workload	Varies by service	33,758	146,702	1,710,242	0.1	154,814,960
Total cost	Dollars	33,758	303,758	563,586	2.0	44,664,036
Personnel cost	Dollars	33,758	195,502	260,841	0	5,618,009
Operational cost	Dollars	33,758	100,618	354,329	0	16,561,950
Investment cost	Dollars	33,758	7,638	132,813	0	22,932,257

Source: GAO.

Notes:

1. Each observation represents the cost of a particular service at a particular post for a particular year. For example, the health care service in Abidjan in 2000 is one observation.

2. Each observation includes data on the name of the post, the units of service provided, and the cost of providing the service.

3. Cost data reflect the total cost of providing a particular service, including both fixed and variable costs. The data also include three components of the total costs: investment cost, personnel cost and operational cost.

4. We excluded observations with a zero workload or zero total cost.

The data contains information on the year the service was provided, the location of the post, and whether the post is standard or "lite" post.[2] Tables 11-14 are frequency tables for the year, location, post type, and ICASS service.

---

[2]The standard cost centers, with 31 services, define the services in more detail than the "lite" cost centers, which bunches some services in broader category and contains 16 services.

Table11: Frequency Table for Year of ICASS Service

Fiscal year	Frequency	Percent	Cumulative percent
2000	3,005	8.90%	8.90%
2001	2,975	8.81	17.71
2002	3,005	8.90	26.62
2003	3,030	8.98	35.59
2004	3,030	8.98	44.57
2005	3,117	9.23	53.80
2006	3,069	9.09	62.89
2007	3,015	8.93	71.82
2008	3,026	8.96	80.79
2009	3,204	9.49	90.28
2010	3,282	9.72	100.00
Total	**33,758**	**100.00%**	

Source: GAO

Table 12: Frequency Table for Type of Post

Post type	Frequency	Percent	Cumulative percent
Lite	12,258	36.31%	36.31%
Standard	21,500	63.69	100.00
Total	**33,758**	**100.00%**	

Source: GAO

Table 13: Frequency Table for Regions

Region	Frequency	Percent	Cumulative percent
Africa	7,423	21.99%	21.99%
East Asia and the Pacific	4,503	13.34	35.33
Europe	9,074	26.88	62.21
International organizations	112	0.33	62.54
Near East	3,955	11.72	74.25
South Asia[a]	842	2.49	76.75
South and Central Asia	776	2.30	79.05
Western Hemisphere	7,073	20.95	100.00
Total	**33,758**	**100.00%**	

Source: GAO.

[a]In 2006, State merged the Office of Central Asian Affairs with the Bureau for South Asian Affairs to create the Bureau for South and Central Asian Affairs.

Table 14: Frequency Table for ICASS Services

ICASS services	Frequency	Percent
Information management technical support	1,627	4.82%
Health services	1,717	5.09
Nonresidential local guard program service	447	1.32
Security services	941	2.79
Vehicle maintenance	663	1.96
Administrative supply	768	2.28
Procurement services	770	2.28
Reproduction services	558	1.65
Shipping and customs	767	2.27
Motor pool services	759	2.25
Nonexpendable property management	768	2.28
Leasing services	768	2.28
Travel	728	2.16
Household furniture, furnishings, and appliance pools	273	0.81
General services[a]	1,029	3.05
Basic package services	1,800	5.33
Pouching services	762	2.26
Mail and messenger services	770	2.28
Reception, switchboard, and telephone services	766	2.27
Information management services[a]	1,026	3.04
Budgets and financial plans	770	2.28
Accounts and records	770	2.28
Payrolling services	770	2.28
Vouchering services	770	2.28
Cashiering services	770	2.28
Financial management services[a]	1,029	3.05
Human resources services[a]	1,028	3.05
Human resources: U.S. citizen services	770	2.28
Human resources: locally employed staff services	770	2.28
Community Liaison Office services	1,664	4.93
Government-owned/long-term lease residential building operations	1,504	4.46
Government-owned/long-term lease nonresidential building operations	1,666	4.94
Short-term lease residential building operations	1,735	5.14
Short-term lease nonresidential building operations	1,374	4.07
Miscellaneous costs	458	1.36

Source: GAO.

Note: The data contain some services not defined in the ICASS standard or lite cost center distribution factors, thus the total shown above is less than 100 percent.

[a]These bundled cost centers are present at posts using the ICASS Lite methodology.

In order to test whether economies of scale exist in providing ICASS services, we used the following specification in the regression:

Ln (unit cost) = $a\_0 + a\_1 * Ln$ (total workload) + a_2 * dummy for region

+ a_3 * dummy for post type + a_4 * dummy for tier

+ a_5 * dummy for services + a_6 * year

Where *total workload* is a measure of units of services provided;

Post type indicates whether a post is a standard or "lite" post;

Tier indicates whether a post is a tier 1 post (USAID and State are colocated);

Year = 1 for 2000, 2 for 2001 and so on.

With large numbers of dummy variables, we ran a stepwise regression, specifying a significance level for removal from the model. In addition to running the regression with the type of services as dummy variables, we also ran the regression on each individual service. For example, we ran a regression on how the unit cost of copying service is related to the number of copies made, where the posts are located, the type of posts and the year the service was provided.

The coefficient on the log of *total workload* can be interpreted as the cost elasticity, a percentage increase in total workload leads to *a_1* percentage change in unit cost. A negative coefficient implies that increased workload is related to decreased unit cost. This model specification has been used in the literature to test for economies of scale.[3] Table 15 presents the regression results from including all the services as dummy variables.

---

[3]For example, in "Does School District Consolidation Cut Costs?" [Duncombe and Yinger, "Does School District Consolidation Cut Costs?" *Education Finance and Policy*, Vol. 2, Is. 4 (Fall 2007)], the authors used a specification of per pupil school spending as a function of school performance, input prices and enrollment. They specified a log linear form to test how per pupil cost is related to the size of enrollment.

Table 15: Summary Regression Results

	Coefficient	T value	P>t
a_0 Constant	7.59	218.34	0.000
a_1 Ln(total workload)	-0.51	-126.22	0.000
a_2 Dummy for region			
_Iregion_2	-0.10	-7.56	0.000
_Iregion_3	0.16	14.18	0.000
_Iregion_4	0.71	10.46	0.000
_Iregion_5	-0.14	-9.97	0.000
_Iregion_6	-0.16	-6.07	0.000
_Iregion_8	-0.19	-16.13	0.000
a_3 Dummy for post type	0.49	37.30	0.000
a_4 Dummy for tier	-0.06	-5.88	0.000
a_5 Dummy for services (30 dummies, not displayed)			
a_6 Year	0.06	47.31	0.000

Source: GAO.

$F_{(45, 33712)} = 9125.46$

Prob > F= 0.0000

R-squared= 0.9241

Adj R-squared= 0.9240

Survey

To obtain agency-level information on customer perceptions on the quality and reasonableness of cost of these ICASS support services overseas, we conducted a web-based survey of a probability sample of ICASS Council representatives who served on an ICASS council at an embassy in fiscals year 2010 or 2011.

The target population consisted of 641 ICASS Council representatives from 8 agencies within the scope of our review—State, USAID, USDA, DOD, Justice, Commerce, DHS, and HHS—in 167 embassies worldwide. We developed our sampling frame from the results of a preliminary survey we sent to ICASS Council chairpersons at 167 posts, requesting the names and e-mail addresses of officials currently serving as ICASS Council representatives at post. We also obtained contact information for ICASS Council Chairs from officials at the ICASS Service Center, State's telephone directory, and officials from customer agencies within the scope of our review. On the basis of our analysis of the results from the preliminary survey, and the information we received from the additional sources mentioned, we determined the data to be adequate for the purposes of providing a sampling frame.

The survey sample design was a simple random sample of 350 ICASS Council representatives selected from the population of 641 ICASS Council representatives. We obtained 184 usable responses for an overall response rate of 53 percent. In addition, we confirmed that 4 of the selected council representatives were out-of-scope for our survey because they retired during the survey period, in 2011. See table 16 for complete response rate data.

Table 16: ICASS Council Representatives That Received and Completed the Survey

Stratum	Population/ universe	Sample size	Responses	Out-of-scope
State	143	85	51	0
USAID	89	54	30	0
Other departments	409	211	103	0
Agriculture	57	31	21	0
Commerce	60	36	13	1
Homeland Security	54	25	10	0
Defense	127	68	30	2
Health and Human Services	34	12	7	0
Justice	77	39	22	1
Total	**641**	**350**	**184**	**4**

Source: GAO.

Nonresponse bias may exist in some survey responses, since characteristics of survey respondents may differ from those of nonrespondents in ways that affect the responses (e.g., if those representing one customer agency would have provided different responses than those that represent another one). We conducted an analysis of our survey results to identify potential sources of nonresponse bias by comparing weighted estimates from respondents to known population values. These values included participation rates, representation by region, and representation by agency. We conducted statistical tests of differences, at the 95 percent confidence level, between estimates and known population values. We did not observe significant differences between weighted estimates and known population values for most of our comparisons. We did, however, observe significant differences in participation rates for seven of the nine ICASS services we included in our survey. Based on the 53 percent response rate and the results of our examination of nonresponse bias in our survey results, we consider the survey results sufficiently reliable for the purposes of this report. However, we chose not to generalize the survey results to the target population of 641 ICASS Council representatives and chose to present the results of our survey for the 184 respondents.

To develop the survey, we interviewed officials from the ICASS Service Center; State's Office of Management, Policy, Rightsizing and Innovation; USAID; and the American Foreign Service Association (AFSA). We also conducted focus groups at U.S. embassies in Manila, Tokyo, Nairobi, and Kigali, with officials from State, USAID, DHS, Commerce, USDA, Justice, DOD, HHS, and locally employed staff. During our visits to these embassies, we also interviewed management counselors and deputy chiefs of mission at all four posts. While we are not able to generalize the results of our focus groups to all overseas personnel of the agencies the participants represented, their responses provided a range of perspectives on the motivations of customers to either obtain support services through ICASS or obtain services outside of the ICASS system. Based on information from our focus groups, observations, and interviews with officials domestically and abroad, we determined ICASS Council representatives to be the most knowledgeable officials in the field to respond to our survey.

We administered the survey between August 8, 2011, and October 25, 2011. We notified 350 ICASS Council representatives through e-mail, which contained information on the review, a unique username and password, and a link to our web-based survey. The instrument included nine services and asked ICASS Council representatives to identify whether or not their agency received the services through ICASS. In order to reduce the burden on respondents of answering questions about

all ICASS services, we only asked questions about nine services.[4] We
selected these nine services based on several factors, such as, the total
cost of the service for fiscal year 2010, ICASS customer satisfaction
ratings, and the number of posts using the service, among others. We
also analyzed the results of our focus groups of customer agency staff in
Manila, Tokyo, Kigali, and Nairobi to develop a list of services that
included both services that customers expressed satisfaction with and
those that customers expressed dissatisfaction with. Next, the survey
instructed respondents to identify significant factors for participating, or
not participating in nine ICASS services; rate the quality of the services
they received through ICASS, or outside of ICASS; rate the importance of
the service to achieving their mission; and to identify how reasonable they
perceived the cost of ICASS services to be, among other questions.

In addition to the reported sampling errors, the practical difficulties of
conducting any survey may introduce other types of errors, commonly
referred to as nonsampling error. For example, differences in how a
particular question is interpreted, the sources of information available to
respondents, or the types of people who do not respond can introduce
unwanted variability into survey results. We included steps in the survey
design, data collection, and data analysis to minimize such nonsampling
errors.

We took steps to clarify questions to ensure that respondents would
correctly interpret survey questions. For example, following our focus
groups in Manila and Tokyo, interviews, and observations in the field, we
designed draft questionnaires in close collaboration with GAO survey
specialists. We conducted pretests in Washington, D.C.—in person or via
e-mail—with former ICASS Council representatives—from Commerce,
DOD, DHS, Justice, USAID, and USDA. We conducted these pretests to
ensure that respondents understood the questions and could provide the
answers; and to ensure that respondents could complete the questions in
a reasonable amount of time. We documented the results of each pretest,
and made revisions to the draft instrument considering feedback from the
pretests. After officially launching the survey, we shared the final survey

---

[4]The nine services included in our survey were furniture pool, motor pool, shipping and
customs, government-owned/long-term lease and short-term lease residential building
operations, vouchering services, leasing services, information management technical
support services, procurement services, and human resources–locally engaged staff
services.

instrument with officials at the ICASS Service Center, and a senior official at State, as a courtesy.

To increase the response rate for this survey, we began contacting non-respondents by e-mail and telephone in several iterations during the data collection period. We developed two follow-up e-mails with log-in information and a link to the survey. To assist us with the follow-up telephone calls, we acquired the services of a professional services for 2 days. After the 2-day period, GAO staff conducted calls from September to October 2011.

An additional source of nonsampling error can be errors in computer processing and data analysis. All computer programs relied upon for analysis of this survey data were independently verified by a second analyst for accuracy.

Customer Satisfaction and Service Delivery Data

To assess customer satisfaction with the quality of ICASS services, we conducted data analyses using data from the annual ICASS Customer Satisfaction survey, which was developed by the ICASS Service Center and contains customer satisfaction scores for ICASS services by overall satisfaction, agency, and service, dating back to 2005. To assess the reliability of the ICASS survey data, we performed manual testing for errors in accuracy and completeness, and discussed data reliability issues with agency officials knowledgeable about the data. Although the results were not generalizeable and we found some issues with the response rates of some groups in the annual satisfaction survey, we determined the data to be sufficiently reliable for the purposes of reporting general levels of satisfaction with ICASS services by customer agency.[5]

---

[5]For example, the ICASS Service Center does not have a list of all eligible respondents to whom they can send the survey invitation. It uses human resources post population data to determine the amount of eligible respondents to the survey and then divides the amount of responses by the survey population to determine a response rate. Respondents anonymously access the survey through a public Web site and have the potential to respond more than once. Because survey administration was anonymous, it is difficult to determine any potential bias in the results. Therefore, the survey results may only reflect the views of the respondents and not those of all ICASS customers.

We also conducted analyses using data from eServices, which was
developed by State's Office of Innovation, and contains service delivery
and customer feedback questionnaire data for fiscal years 2010 and
2011.

Appendix II: Services Available through ICASS

Dozens of specific administrative services are provided through ICASS, and these services are bundled into so-called "cost centers." Table 17 lists these cost centers and provides a description of the services provides within each bundle.

Table 17: ICASS Cost Centers

Cost center	Description
Information management technical support	Provides the installation and maintenance of hardware/software, training, e-mail systems, system security operations and programs, system backup, information technology recommendations for software/hardware updates and changes, and troubleshooting services.
Health services	Services vary depending on the post and the staffing of the Health Unit but may include: first aid, immunizations, coordination with and evaluation of local caregivers, support with medical evacuations and hospitalizations, and other similar services of a health operation.
Nonresidential local guard program service	Pertains only to guard services at shared buildings such as chanceries, embassy compounds, and annexes. The service includes appropriate screening of visitors and vehicles.
Security services	Service includes conducting special investigations and background investigations for locally employed staff, reviewing and recommending security enhancements for nonresidential spaces, taking security photos, fingerprinting new locally employed staff, and assisting with general security issues.
Vehicle maintenance	Service includes routine maintenance of official vehicles and related record keeping and coordination with local vendors for nonroutine repairs.
Administrative supply	Orders and dispenses office supplies. Includes inventory control, warehousing, and issuance of office supplies.
Procurement services	Manages purchase of items or services for official use only. This includes purchase by contract, purchase order, requisition, credit card and other standard means.
Reproduction services	Provides printing and copying services through a central facility.
Shipping and customs	This service varies from post to post but may include arranging and overseeing (as required) the packing, crating and forwarding of shipments, and performing necessary customs clearance for all incoming and outgoing shipments (e.g., official shipments, household effects, vehicles, pouches, equipment, etc.).
Motor pool services	Covers the scheduling, dispatch and proper use of official vehicles. Includes providing skilled, knowledgeable drivers and proper upkeep of vehicles.
Nonexpendable property management	Covers inventory management, warehousing and issuance of office and residential furniture, furnishings and appliances.
Leasing services	Includes all phases of the leasing process for residential, office, warehouse or other space as required by requesting agency. Pertains to U.S. government-signed leases only. Includes locating appropriate, safe properties, negotiating and renewing leases, monitoring landlord performance, and providing assistance with initial connection and termination of utility and phone services.
Travel	Services may differ from post to post but may include: processing flight, ground transportation, and hotel reservation requests; assisting with arrival and departure; overseeing travel management center contractor; and obtaining visas.
Household furniture, furnishings, and appliance pools	Includes requisitioning, inventory control, warehousing, care, delivery, removal and disposal of all pooled furniture and appliances.

Cost center	Description
Basic package services	Varies by post but covers the basic services that support all agencies such as accreditation, licenses and permits, the post report, telephone books, support for/liaison with local international school(s), negotiation of hotel rates, support structure for VIP visits, surveys for cost of living allowance, per diem and education allowance, coordination of newcomer and temporary staff orientation, coordination of the mission awards program, provision of building access badges, and other such services.
Pouching services	Covers the receipt and distribution of incoming pouch materials and the preparation and forwarding of outgoing pouches (classified and unclassified).
Mail and messenger services	Covers pickup, delivery, and sorting of mail from various sources. Includes transport of mail to and from airport, coordination with local customs and airline personnel, and receipt and delivery of registered and express delivery. Also provides local messenger service.
Reception, switchboard, and telephone services	Covers post's central switchboard services and reception services for visitors. Includes answering and directing calls within mission offices, servicing and relocating of instruments connected to the switchboard, and support for official cell phone program, where applicable.
Budgets and financial plans	Includes the preparation and submission of budgets that meet deadlines and reflect customer needs based on trends, analysis and customer input. Provides financial advice including assistance to the ICASS council and Budget Committee regarding ICASS financial and budget issues.
Accounts and records	Manages allotments of participating serviced agencies (i.e., agencies whose accounting records are maintained by Resources Management/Global Financial Services Charleston) recording, reviewing, and adjusting obligations and certifying funds available.
Payrolling services	Payrolling services involves reporting and maintenance of time and attendance, pay, benefits, leave allowances, and tax records; coordinates periodic payments for locally employed staff; reports locally employed staff retirement/insurance plans to host government; and follows up on lost payroll checks and reconciles payroll problems with payment center.
Vouchering services	Vouchering services prepares, certifies and tracks vouchers, ensuring timely payments to vendors and other U.S. government agencies. It maintains controls to preclude duplicate payments and legal records of payments. Also assists with preparing Travel Vouchers.
Cashiering services	Cashier services includes petty cash advances, check cashing and accommodation exchange (at posts where it is authorized). Collects receipts from sales of official property and receipts for personal usage of certain services (i.e., gasoline and telephone).
Human resources: U.S. citizen services	Provides all human resources services including employee relations, evaluations, career advancement, discipline and grievances, and advising on health/life insurance, retirement plan, Thrift Savings Plan and other allotments. It also includes maintaining employee organization, position and staffing plans (Note: The latter services related to maintaining mission-wide reports and staffing plans are covered under Basic Package).
Human resources: locally employed staff services	Manages the compensation plan, salary surveys, position classifications, awards program, locally employed staff employee orientation, and job advertisements. If you do not have locally employed staff employees, then you do not receive this service.
Community Liaison Office services	Provides a wide range of community integrating functions including but not limited to welcome packages, orientation seminars, school interface, briefings, and post newsletters. The Community Liaison Office maintains community interface with host country organizations.

Cost center	Description
Government-owned/long-term lease residential building operations	Provides routine maintenance and preventative repairs, ensures preparation for new arrivals, and ensures adequate utilities (garbage removal, heating and air conditioning) are available to the extent possible. Service may be provided directly by ICASS or involve working with the landlord. Includes maintenance of grounds if government-owned.
Government-owned/long-term lease nonresidential building operations	Provides routine maintenance and preventative repairs, manages custodial and grounds services, plans space utilization, and ensures adequate utilities (garbage removal, heating and air-conditioning) are available to the extent possible. Service may be provided directly by ICASS or involve working with the landlord.
Short-term lease residential building operations	This service covers all activities related to occupancy and use of short-term leased residential properties. Landlord responsibilities vary from post to post (both in practice and according to local law) and it may be necessary to adjust the kinds of services provided by the mission based on local conditions. The services include: (1) work with the landlord to ensure reasonable and necessary repairs are made properly and on time and/or performing minor repairs with contractors or in-house staff, as appropriate; (2) ensure properties are prepared for new arrivals, conduct preoccupancy and pre-departure inspections and perform routine between occupant fix-ups (e.g., painting, minor repairs); (3) provide residential "hospitality/welcome kits" in accordance with post policy; (4) provide security escort services for maintenance personnel in accordance with post policy; and (5) repair/reupholster government-owned furniture and equipment in accordance with post policy.
Short-term lease nonresidential building operations	This service covers all activities related to occupancy and use of shared short-term lease nonresidential properties and includes: (1) work with the landlord to ensure reasonable and necessary repairs are made properly and on time, the building infrastructure and grounds are properly maintained and/or perform minor repairs with contractors or in-house staff, as appropriate; (2) provide or contract for custodial services; (3) perform routine between occupant "fix-up" and prepare for new arrivals; (4) provide security escort services for maintenance personnel as required, in accordance with post policy; and (5) repair/reupholster government-owned furniture and equipment in accordance with post policy.
Miscellaneous costs	This includes only those costs that are not easily spread to other specific services, or of minimal value compared to the effort and expense to spread the costs precisely. The total for miscellaneous costs generally should not exceed five percent of the total ICASS budget.
Financial management services[a]	Includes services provided under the following ICASS Standard cost centers: budget and financial plans, accounts and records, payrolling, vouchering, and cashiering.
General services[a]	Includes services provided under the following ICASS Standard cost centers: vehicle maintenance, administrative supply, procurement, reproduction, shipping and customs, motor pool, nonexpendable property management, leasing, and travel.
Information management services[a]	Includes services provided under the following ICASS Standard cost centers: pouching; mail and messenger services; and reception, switchboard, and telephone services.
Human resources services[a]	Includes services provided under the following ICASS Standard cost centers: human resources–U.S. citizen services, and human resources–locally employed staff services.

Source: State.

[a]These bundled cost centers are present at posts using the ICASS "Lite" methodology.

Appendix III: Status of Consolidation of State and USAID Administrative Platforms

USAID has significantly increased its participation in ICASS services since it began systematically consolidating its operations with State overseas. In 2006, recognizing the need to contain growth and eliminate duplicative and non-essential government functions at overseas posts, State and USAID issued a joint strategic vision for management operations to guide the consolidation of administrative support services. This strategic vision called for a leaner, more flexible and more responsive administrative platform to provide services to all ICASS customers, at better value to the U.S. taxpayer and at cost savings to both State and USAID. The issuance of this strategic vision followed pilot consolidation projects at four posts, whose goal was to combine the best employees, equipment, and processes from existing operations to ensure that both State and USAID, as well as all ICASS customers, benefited from improved services at lower cost to the taxpayer. Following this pilot project, State and USAID reported that the four posts had successfully consolidated in full or in part 12 of the 16 services targeted, resulting in operational efficiencies and avoided costs.

Since 2007, following this pilot project, State and USAID have been consolidating administrative support services overseas in order to improve the efficiency and effectiveness of management operations. State and USAID divided posts into three tiers, based on when the two agencies expected to colocate on a new embassy compound, and began consolidating operations at posts which were colocated the earliest. The two agencies first consolidated 15 services at so-called Tier 1 posts, where State and USAID were colocated on a new embassy compound by fiscal year 2007. By October 2007, 33 such posts had consolidated many or all of the targeted services. According to State, another 14 posts in Tier 2—where posts were expected to be colocated on a new embassy compound in fiscal year 2008, 2009, or 2010—had consolidated 70 percent of available services by October 2010. State and USAID are currently reviewing the status of consolidation at Tier 3 posts—those expected to be colocated in fiscal year 2011 or later. Going forward, State and USAID will continue to obtain services through ICASS. In 2009 guidance regarding further consolidation, State and USAID advised posts that when new offices are opened or existing programs are expanded, the default plan should be to purchase the necessary support service from ICASS rather than to set up or expand parallel support systems.

In 2011, State and USAID established a Joint Management Board to facilitate further consolidation of services and ensure that customers of these services receive high quality administrative support at a reasonable cost. A joint State-USAID task force supporting the Quadrennial

Diplomacy and Development Review, Task Force 11, recommended this board be created to solve management issues, communicate to the field with a single voice, and implement change.[1] Task Force 11 also recommended that the Joint Management Board formulate a consolidation policy for State and USAID, including establishing clear criteria for exceptions to consolidation, weighing the need for a single platform overseas to achieve cost effective, high quality services with post-specific situations where the embassy and the USAID mission believe that a strong basis exists for flexibility in consolidation of some services. According to board members, one of the board's initial tasks is to improve communication about consolidation and provide further guidance to posts in an effort to mitigate USAID concerns.

---

[1]Department of State and the U.S. Agency for International Development, *Leading Through Civilian Power: The First Quadrennial Diplomacy and Development Review* (Washington, D.C.: Dec. 15, 2010).

Appendix IV: Agency Participation in ICASS

We analyzed data from State to determine participation rates in ICASS. Table 18 shows participation rates for all non-State subagency codes present at 10 or more posts overseas in fiscal year 2011.[1] We calculated these rates by: (1) determining which posts each subagency was present at; (2) determining how many cost centers were available at those posts; and (3) determining the number of cost centers the subagency participated in. The participation rates listed below show the percentage of cost centers each subagency participated in 2005 and 2011 of the total cost centers available at posts where it has a presence.

Table 18: Rate of Participation in Available Services, by Agency, 2005 and 2011[a]

	2005		2011	
Subagency name	Rate	Posts[b]	Rate	Posts[b]
Navy Personnel Exchange Program	29%	15	16%	11
Army–Deputy Chief of Staff (Personnel), Students At Foreign Civilian Schools	16	7	17	18
Broadcasting Board of Governors–Correspondent Bureaus	21	15	18	12
Air Force–U.S. Air Force Students	22	14	21	22
Air Force–Professional Exchange Program	21	19	21	14
U.S. Marine Corps	21	14	27	25
American Battle Monuments Commission	27	11	31	10
National Geospatial Agency	31	10	32	12
Army–Deputy Chief of Staff (Operations), Strategic Leadership Division	33	57	34	49
Peace Corps	34	69	36	69
Immigration and Customs Enforcement/Container Security Initiative Special Investigations			37	10
Centers for Disease Control and Prevention–Detailees to International Organizations	45	3	38	17
Broadcasting Board of Governors–Transmitting Stations	40	11	41	10
Treasury–Office of International Affairs, Office of Technical Assistance	32	25	42	30
Naval Health Research Center	43	2	43	28
Army–U.S. Southern Command Traditional Commander-in-Charge Activities	34	21	44	20

[1]Individual agencies may have multiple sub-agency codes for ICASS billing purposes, and participation rates generally vary by sub-agency code, even within the same agency. In some cases, these sub-agency codes correspond to a discrete unit within an agency, such as the Defense Intelligence Agency. In others, the codes correspond to accounting entities, such as USAID's Operating Expenses account. In 2011, there were 320 such sub-agency codes in ICASS. DOD had the most codes (152) while the other agencies within the scope of our review had between 8 and 56 codes. As a result, it is not feasible or meaningful to calculate an overall agency-wide participation rate, and the figures we present here are at the sub-agency code level.

Subagency name	2005		2011	
	Rate	Posts[b]	Rate	Posts[b]
Customs and Border Protection–Container Security Initiative	40	16	45	40
Open Source Center	41	26	46	31
U.S. Coast Guard	49	7	48	14
USAID–International Disaster Assistance	44	13	49	18
Library of Congress	49	14	50	14
Army–U.S. Southern Command, Counter Drug Teams	54	20	51	28
U.S. Army Corps of Engineers	52	13	51	13
Navy Investigative Services	31	4	51	10
Centers for Disease Control and Prevention	55	35	53	34
USAID–Child Survival & Diseases Program Fund	30	18	54	26
U.S. Secret Service	52	20	55	25
Justice–International Criminal Investigative Training and Assistance Program	54	9	55	21
USAID–Office of Transition Initiatives	45	7	55	12
USAID–Operating Expenses, Regional Organizations	53	8	55	10
USAID–Development Assistance	37	49	56	54
Animal and Plant Health Inspection Service	53	42	56	47
Army–U.S. Africa Command			56	28
Department of Energy–Moscow/Kiev/Tokyo/Beijing/Vienna	65	6	56	13
U.S. Africa Command–Regional Defense Cooperation Office			56	12
Air Force–U.S. Central Command Operations and Maintenance	45	10	56	11
Army–U.S. European Command	51	37	57	37
Federal Aviation Administration	56	13	57	20
Internal Revenue Service	63	13	57	15
Social Security Administration	56	27	58	26
USAID–Economic Support Funds	34	17	58	21
Customs and Border Protection–International Affairs Office	47	11	59	26
U.S. Citizenship and Immigration Services–Refugee, Asylum, and International Operations	68	46	60	42
USAID–President's Emergency Plan for AIDS Relief, Program Staff Support			61	19
Centers for Disease Control and Prevention–Global AIDS Program	54	7	62	49
Treasury–Office of International Affairs	53	7	62	12
Defense Threat Reduction Agency	50	11	62	10
Justice–Overseas Prosecutorial Development Assistance and Training	73	4	63	19
Navy–Force Protection Detachment	63	8	63	17
USAID–Freedom Support Act	44	16	63	15
Foreign Agricultural Service	66	82	64	76
Transportation Security Administration	62	16	64	24

GAO-12-317 Embassy Management

Subagency name	2005		2011	
	Rate	Posts[b]	Rate	Posts[b]
Defense Security Cooperation Agency	66	113	66	122
Army–U.S. Southern Command, Security Assistance Officers	57	23	66	24
Foreign Agriculture Service/Agricultural Trade Office	54	20	66	16
Federal Bureau of Investigation/ Legal Attaché	65	68	67	85
Army–Force Protection Detachment	65	5	67	12
USAID–Operating Expenses, Missions	51	87	68	88
Justice–Criminal Division	58	19	68	16
Drug Enforcement Administration	74	72	70	84
Immigration and Customs Enforcement–International Affairs Office	65	45	70	59
Foreign Commercial Service	68	112	71	106
Food and Drug Administration	18	1	75	11
Millennium Challenge Corporation			76	19
Defense Intelligence Agency	82	146	81	147

Source: GAO analysis of ICASS data.

[a]In some instances, nonparticipation may indicate that a service is not offered to all agencies at a post or that an agency does not need a particular service. In such instances, nonparticipation does not necessarily indicate duplication of services.

[b]We calculated the number of posts an agency subcode was present at using data from the ICASS Global Database. If ICASS charged an agency subcode for at least one service at a given post, we determined that that subcode was present at that post.

Appendix V: Comments from the Department of State

United States Department of State

Chief Financial Officer

Washington, D.C. 20520

JAN 2 6 2012

Mr. Loren Yager
Managing Director
International Affairs and Trade
Government Accountability Office
441 G Street, N.W.
Washington, D.C. 20548-0001

Dear Mr. Yager:

We appreciate the opportunity to review your draft report, "EMBASSY MANAGEMENT: Agencies Missing Cost Savings Opportunities by Continuing to Duplicate Overseas Support Services," GAO Job Code 320802.

The enclosed Department of State comments are provided for incorporation with this letter as an appendix to the final report.

If you have any questions concerning this response, please contact James Core, Senior Management Analyst, Office of Management Policy, Rightsizing and Innovation at (202) 647-1068.

Sincerely,

James L. Millette

cc: GAO – Michael J. Courts
M/PRI– William Haugh
State/OIG – Evelyn Klemstine

Department of State Comments on GAO Draft Report
EMBASSY MANAGEMENT: Agencies Missing Cost Savings Opportunities
by Continuing to Duplicate Overseas Support Services
(GAO-12-317, GAO Code 320802)

Thank you for the opportunity to comment on your draft report entitled *"Embassy
Management: Agencies Missing Cost Savings Opportunities by Continuing to
Duplicate Overseas Support Services."*

The Department, as both the principal International Cooperative Administrative
Support Services (ICASS) service provider and the largest customer of ICASS
system services, is firmly committed to an efficient and effective overseas
administrative shared-services platform. We recognize that a well-managed,
consolidated administrative platform furthers our ability - and the ability of the
United States government as a whole - to successfully implement our foreign
policy objectives and contain overall cost and presence. We believe the draft
report overwhelmingly supports these facts and the conclusion that there are
opportunities to further consolidate overseas support services. We welcome the
opportunity to further assess how the USG can attain greater efficiencies and
economies of scale at our missions abroad.

ICASS is now going on its 14th year as the shared administrative services platform.
Working with our interagency ICASS customers and partners at posts and the
Washington level, we continue to make improvements in ensuring we meet the
cost of doing business globally in the most transparent and prudent way possible.
As the principal ICASS service provider, we understand our fiduciary
responsibility to provide high quality, cost-effective services to the interagency
community, while striving to continually contain the cost to the taxpayer.

To that end, the Department invests significant resources in ensuring that ICASS
budgeting and oversight processes are transparent, collaborative, and emphasize
the empowerment of ICASS councils and budget committees at post. For example,
the Department facilitates a data driven process of counting agency workload,
preparing budgets, and presenting invoices that are approved by customer agencies
at post and then by agency representatives in Washington. Further, the Department
- through activities largely funded by its own appropriated dollars and at no cost to
customer agencies – invests in technology and supports a quality management
program to assist the customer-led ICASS councils that have responsibility for

2

overseeing local service delivery as outlined in the Foreign Affairs Handbook (FAH), specifically 6 FAH-5 H-222.3-4.

While we support the general conclusion of the report, the Department does have a number of conceptual suggestions for consideration which are discussed in the sections below.

<u>Nonparticipation in ICASS Services Indicates Potential Duplication</u>

Recommendation: Congress may wish to consider requiring agencies to participate in ICASS services unless they provide a business case to show that they can obtain these services outside of ICASS without increasing overall costs to the U.S. government or that the mission cannot be achieved within ICASS.

Response: The Department concurs with the proposed recommendation to Congress. The Department concurs with the study's conclusion that there is unnecessary duplication of services incurring unnecessary expense to the taxpayer when agencies establish duplicative service arrangements

<u>State Has Made Little Progress on Other Cost Containment Efforts</u>

Recommendation: The Secretary of State should continue efforts to reengineer administrative processes and seek innovative managerial approaches that would reduce the need for American administrative staff overseas.

See comment 1.

Response: The Department partially concurs with the recommendation. We support the view that reengineering processes and developing innovative solutions are activities that are continual in nature in order to improve service and the cost effectiveness of its delivery. However, we do not agree with the premise that such actions have not been undertaken or will substantially reduce the need for number of American management staff abroad. Further, the finding that "costs per unit of output have generally decreased" for 28 services over the last ten years is clear evidence that the Department has made progress on cost containment. Economies of scale are not inherently self-generating – they reflect a broad range of efforts to constrain both fixed and variable costs. These efforts are led by the American managers of the ICASS system at post. We encourage GAO to reassess this recommendation and offer additional information below for consideration.

For example, analysis of the staffing pattern reveals a lean management platform with just 1,201 U.S. direct hire management (USDH) professionals supervising

3

27,872 locally engaged ICASS staff at 167 missions worldwide. These USDH ICASS management professionals provide services for themselves, another 31,513 locally employed (LE) staff and 21,708 USG officials from 45 agencies and 27,100 dependents. Also, it should be noted that while the number of ICASS customers increased from 15,736 in FY2000 to 22,909 in FY2011, an increase of 46 percent, the number of service providers only increased from 885 to 1,201 or an increase of 36 percent.

See comment 2.

It is not the view of State's leadership that "significant ICASS cost savings are elusive unless State reduces the number of management-related American staff overseas." Analysis of the ICASS budget reveals that American salaries and position support costs are not as large a cost driver as some interagency stakeholders believe. In FY 2011, salaries and support costs for ICASS-funded American positions comprised approximately14 percent of all ICASS expenses. While we continually assess our global footprint, the Department must ensure that the U.S. government has the management capability needed to implement the 21st century statecraft conducted from our diplomatic platforms abroad. As part of the Secretary's "Diplomacy 3.0" initiative, additional management staff were targeted to posts experiencing the greatest increase in ICASS workload.

See comment 2.

Given that our American USDH ICASS personnel are just 14 percent of ICASS expenditures, cuts in ICASS USDHs are unlikely to result in "significant" savings. However, cuts to significantly reduce this corps of management professionals would degrade internal controls and oversight in overseas environments. We believe that significant reductions in USDH ICASS positions would jeopardize the Department's ability to maintain a global diplomatic platform that is flexible enough to support our foreign policy goals and the missions of ICASS customer agencies – often conducted in very challenging environments. American management positions are critical to reducing and remediating billing errors, which the report notes as an ongoing customer concern.

See comment 3.

The Department challenges a statement on page 18 about the use of training slots. The GAO, quoting an official from a customer agency at an unnamed post, writes that a Deputy Management Counselor was assigned to the post "for training", noting an opinion that the Deputy's services were not required. This is incorrect. In-depth training of officers occurs at the Foreign Service Institute in Arlington, Virginia most commonly before assignments. No positions at post are added as "training opportunities."

4

Deputy Management Counselors are assigned only at the largest, most complex
overseas locations, five of which host multiple missions, e.g., Paris, Brussels,
Rome, Vienna, and Nairobi. There are 19 Deputy Management Counselor
positions at overseas posts and none of these are "training" positions. The
Department is convinced that assignment of a Deputy Management Counselor at
these posts is appropriate and that an analysis of staffing, workload and complexity
at any post with a Deputy Management Counselor would disprove this anecdote.

<u>State Has Not Implemented Systemic Innovation and Reengineering of Service
Delivery</u>

See comment 4.

The report would have benefited from additional examination of the Department's
efforts to streamline services, contain cost, and improve quality. Further
interviews with the Department's management bureaus would have revealed a
more complete story and perspectives unavailable to other agencies and staff in the
field. While the anecdotes contained in the draft report may be germane to that
post's operations, they are not necessarily representative of the global platform.
The Department must implement processes and systems that can be replicated
worldwide in heterogeneous environments – often isolated - and in extremely
challenging technical and physical conditions. Unlike most other ICASS agencies,
our efforts must be sustainable around the world. This investment of time to
deploy rigorously tested solutions produces tools that are more useful for long term
process improvement across the enterprise.

The Department has worked to institutionalize a culture of continuous management
improvement through business process reengineering, improving our human
capital, harnessing technology and introducing world-wide collaboration of
American and locally engaged management professionals.

The following accomplishments highlight some of the innovations of the past
several years that illustrate how careful planning and deployment delivers
reengineered services that benefit the Department and ICASS customer agencies:

1. **Collaborative Management Initiative (CMI)**: In 2008, the Department
   standardized post-specific business processes with the launch of the first
   worldwide CMI playbook for 95 administrative services. In 2011, the
   Department optimized delivery routines for 97 services. CMI is field-
   driven with a worldwide network of 204 quality coordinators who support
   innovation and quality management at 252 posts. CMI specifically is an
   example of the Department's efforts to involve all posts in a common

5

collaboration to set goals, share methods of improvement, measure satisfaction, and contain costs.

2. **eServices Performance Dashboard:** The Department maintains an interactive dashboard that depicts a high-level overview of the data generated by eServices in a series of graphs and tables, allowing a comparison of each post's performance in providing service against the Uniform Service Standards (USS), to other posts in its region, its bureau and department-wide. Everyone with OpenNet access can view the dashboard.

3. **Processing Service Requests:** In 2012, the Department will begin to field a second generation version of "eServices" that provides a common look and feel for customers requesting ICASS services, and will give managers real-time performance metrics. The results will be reflected in the new eServices software that is launching in 2012; it will be available from State's OpenNet and the internet.

4. **Financial Systems**: The Department has implemented ISO 9001 certified voucher processing systems and deployed an integrated reporting tool that provides posts and ICASS customer agencies the ability to view, sort, and manage their financial management data and workload counts.

5. **Financial Services:** The Department expanded the centralization of financial processing from posts by providing low-cost, quality vouchering services to all posts. Post Support Unit (PSU) now services more than 90 posts, worldwide, with efficient and consistent vouchering services from 3 central locations. The Department is now providing 24-hr support to customers around the globe leveraging low-cost operations in Bangkok and Sofia.

6. **Procurement Management:** The Department has also implemented a standard worldwide procurement program which allows procurements to be initiated and processed from alternate locations. This has been especially helpful for high danger posts, such as Iraq, where much of the procurement work is not done at post.

7. **Inventory Management**: The Department now has a centralized worldwide inventory system that will facilitate the analysis of numerous programs.

8. **Logistics Management:** The Department introduced several new programs that have streamlined and enhanced numerous business processes. For example, employees can now initiate and track their household effects shipments, posts can track official shipments, supplies can be pre-positioned overseas to reduce shipping times as well as reduce secure procurement acquisition times from 18 months to six or less.

9. **Pouch:** The Department has deployed new technology that allows for the tracking of classified and unclassified pouches in the supply chain at any

6

time. This has allowed the Department to collect and analyze data on this $30M program to determine the most cost effective shipping routes and ensure the best service to posts at the lowest possible cost.

10. **Local Guard Program**: The Department centralized contract award and administration of the worldwide local guard program, relieving post GSO's of one of the most burdensome aspects of post procurements and increasing economies of scale and improving oversight.

11. **Energy Management**: In 2011, the Department deployed a global network energy management program that reduced energy consumption by almost $900,000 within ten months of launch.

12. **IT Management**: The Global IT Modernization program standardizes the Department's IT resources and the refreshment process for the Department and customer agencies abroad.

13. **Leveraging Web-based Tools**: The Department uses web-technology to improve service delivery. The Department deployed a Knowledge Base tool – a repository of over 2,000 financial management frequently-asked questions and how-to's, which are accessed over 100,000 times a year by customers. In 2011, The Department conducted 105 webinars with 367 subject matter experts worldwide to develop optimized delivery routines for the most requested ICASS services.

Performance Metrics Do Not Address Some Aspects of ICASS Customer Dissatisfaction

Recommendation: The Secretary of State should develop additional uniform service standards and other performance measures that gauge ICASS service providers' progress in resolving major sources of customer dissatisfaction.

Response: The Department partially concurs with the recommendation and we believe that it must be expanded to include the active participation of customer agencies. We agree with the premise of the recommendation as demonstrated by the Department's ongoing effort to develop the next generation quality management system that is being deployed in 2012. As the auditing team is aware, the Department launched a quality management program in 2006 that includes quality managers at each post.

At a series of workshops between 2006 and 2008, representatives from a wide variety of posts and customers developed USS for each cost center and each subcomponent of each cost center. These workshops were initiated and funded by

7

State and were based on the newly developed (and completely reworked) ICASS handbook which was itself an interagency project that was initiated by State to improve our ability to measure services and deliver them more uniformly at every post.

The process for setting the Uniform Service Standards included customer agency representatives in addition to a two month vetting to the field for comments. The ability for customers to provide feedback on the services they receive for every transaction is part of the existing eServices tool and will be enhanced in the new system. This information is presently being used by post management sections to address customer concerns, identify problematic areas, and improve processes.

As briefed to the GAO on September 29, this initiative is being expanded in Spring 2012 with the launch of an updated online request tracking and business analytics tool. At this time, USS performance data is collected for the most commonly used services. The new system architecture to be released in 2012 will increase our capability to capture and report performance data and make use of business analytics tools. Some features of the new system include tracking performance metrics for individual agencies, increasing the services for which performance data and customer satisfaction is collected, and increasing the data points available for service managers. The Department will soon have data that can be used to recalibrate existing service standards and develop new standards for other services.

See comment 5.

The Department believes that the GAO commentary and recommendation on this topic is incomplete. A meaningful discussion of customer satisfaction must call for greater participation from ICASS customer agencies at post. Customer feedback is vital to the management team at post. The Department believes that it is important to hear from agency representatives about the services that they consider "problematic" so that concerns can be addressed.

The ICASS Executive Board, recognizing that participation was inconsistent at the local level, took action in 2010 and 2011 to encourage more engagement at the post level. The ICASS Executive Board and the FAH both underscore the importance of effective Council participation in ensuring that ICASS services are appropriate for local conditions. The ICASS Customer Satisfaction Survey, eServices Survey Data, and annual Assessment of ICASS Services are existing tools that require active local engagement to be meaningful.

8

<u>Restricted Use of Alternate ICASS Service Providers (ASP) Limits Opportunities
for Greater Efficiencies</u>

Recommendation: Where agencies are able to demonstrate, through a compelling
business case, that they can provide a service more efficiently than the existing
State ICASS provider without adverse effects on the overall government budget,
the ICASS Executive Board and the Joint Management Board allow the creation of
new ICASS service providers, in lieu of State, that could provide administrative
services to the other agencies at individual posts.

See comment 6.

Response: We support the establishment of additional ASPs if a provider other
than State can demonstrate efficiencies and savings for the USG and provide the
service for all customers at post at price points that are acceptable without creating
additional duplication or service interruptions. There are no restrictions on any
agency other than State being an ASP; the only requirement is that the ASP must
provide the particular ICASS service to all agencies. Duplication of effort, as the
GAO has noted in its report, is not the way to proceed.

The following are GAO's comments on the Department of State's letter
dated January 26, 2012.

GAO Comments

1. As State and USAID continue to consolidate their administrative
   operations overseas, we believe that opportunities exist to reduce the
   number of American management staff by making greater use of local
   staff. However, we agree with State that efforts to reengineer
   administrative processes encompass a variety of actions, not limited
   to reducing the need for American administrative staff, and have
   clarified our recommendation accordingly.

2. We believe that the cost of American management positions oversees
   is significant, even at 14 percent of all ICASS expenses, which totaled
   over $2 billion is fiscal year 2011. Thus, reductions in this staffing
   could have significant cost implications for ICASS participating
   agencies and the U.S. government overall.

3. We have removed this statement from our report.

4. The draft report mentioned some of State's efforts to improve the
   quality of ICASS services. We have updated our report to include
   additional efforts that State has noted, along with the cost savings
   associated with these efforts.

5. We revised the report and recommendation to emphasize the
   importance of customer agency participation in the development of
   service standards.

6. In 2006, the State-USAID Joint Management Council, the
   predecessor to the Joint Management Board, sent guidance to posts
   instructing them not to initiate any new Alternative Service Providers
   at posts that were expected to have consolidated administrative
   operations by 2010. ICASS and USAID officials we spoke to consider
   this policy a restriction on the creation of new Alternative Service
   Providers. However, we have re-directed this recommendation from
   the ICASS Executive Board to the Secretary of State and the
   Administrator of USAID, as their agencies comprise the Joint
   Management Board.

Appendix VI: Comments from the U.S. Agency for International Development

January 25, 2012

Michael J. Courts
A-Director, International Affairs and Trade
U.S. Government Accountability Office
Washington, DC 20548

Dear Mr. Courts:

I am pleased to provide the formal response to the Government Accountability Office (GAO) draft report entitled "EMBASSY MANAGEMENT: Agencies Missing Cost Saving Opportunities by Continuing to Duplicate Overseas Support Services" (GAO-12-317 for the U.S. Agency for International Development (USAID).

The enclosed USAID comments are provided for incorporation with this letter as an appendix to the final report.

Thank you for the opportunity to respond to the GAO draft report and for the courtesies extended by your staff in the conduct of this audit review.

Sincerely,

Angelique M. Crumbly /s/
Acting Assistant to the Administrator
Bureau for Management
U.S. Agency for International Development

Enclosure: a/s

- 3 -

USAID COMMENTS ON GAO DRAFT REPORT - EMBASSY MANAGEMENT:
Agencies Missing Cost Saving Opportunities by Continuing to Duplicate Overseas Support
Services (GAO-12-317)

USAID believes that GAO's report is a balanced look at some of the challenges International
Cooperative Administrative Support Services (ICASS) faces in its attempts to provide high
quality services at reasonable costs. Our response focuses on specific areas of great interest
to USAID management.

Duplication of Services: The report indicates that agencies can likely achieve lower overall
costs for the U.S. Government by greater subscription to ICASS and eliminating duplication
of service provider platforms. USAID agrees with this observation and demonstrated its
commitment to reducing duplication through consolidation of 12 ICASS cost centers at all
collocated posts (tier one posts) beginning in FY 2008. USAID and State also agreed to
cooperate in areas outside of ICASS as well, such as greater participation in eligible family
employment and at-post language training. This effort expanded to other posts in FY 2009
and FY 2010 (tier two posts) as further collocation of USAID into new embassy compounds
occurred. In August 2009, USAID and State agreed that remaining non-collocated posts (tier
three posts) should also consolidate the agreed upon services under ICASS by the beginning
of FY 2011 or present waiver requests to maintain separate services to a joint USAID/State
committee. These efforts have collectively resulted in USAID participation in 93 percent of
non-waived cost centers in tier one posts, 91 percent of tier two posts and 80 percent of tier
three posts as of December 2011.

As noted in the GAO report, USAID and State agreed as part of the Quadrennial Diplomacy
and Development Review to establish a Joint Management Board (JMB). This board just
issued a cable to all posts indicating the Secretary of State's and USAID Administrator's
commitment to (1) complete the consolidation of agreed upon services, and (2) prepare
business case analyses of other management services that could offer further opportunities
for consolidation. A major initiative relating to consolidation of USAID's information
technology platform is already underway and will be piloted at three posts beginning January
2012.

USAID management is committed to pushing the limits of consolidation of services provided
that service quality is maintained or improved, USAID's overall costs do not increase
substantially, and USAID's ability to carry out its programmatic responsibilities are not
compromised.

USAID takes the position that if other agencies are more forcefully encouraged to sign up for
more ICASS services there are cost containment actions the ICASS system should
incorporate that could be a prelude to more voluntary participation. We think this is
important because the GAO report indicates that greater ICASS participation will lower costs
because the fixed cost components will be spread over more users. However, we do believe
that State can set a good example for other agencies by thoroughly examining whether
internal State operations, such as its Bureau of International Narcotics and Law Enforcement

- 4 -

(INL) can take steps to join motor pool operations. To the extent INL's operations are collocated within embassy service provider boundaries, consolidation in ICASS motor pools can save the U.S. Government money and demonstrate to other customers with law enforcement missions that ICASS has the capacity to provide key services to agencies whose operational requirements are relatively unpredictable.

ICASS Cost Containment: Many customer agencies noted in their interviews with GAO that they have serious concerns with rapidly escalating costs under ICASS. USAID agrees and believes that simply expanding the ICASS customer base does not get at the heart of needed cost reductions. State should move aggressively and rapidly toward regionalization of services, pursue outsourcing opportunities, rationalize its local employee workforce, and seek to empower local employees to assume duties presently occupied by very expensive American personnel. As noted by GAO, some of these initiatives with very promising cost returns have stalled because they were determined to be administratively burdensome. USAID had to overcome similar logic to accept the premise that some of its self-provided services could be fulfilled by subscribing to ICASS. We believe that State needs to fight internal forces of inertia vigorously to make changes rapidly to its current model of service provision. In the current budget environment, USAID and other agencies' budgets for program implementation are being squeezed by ICASS cost increases. Also, implementing a strong cost containment effort could lead to greater participation which would lead to even lower ICASS cost because, as mentioned, the fixed cost would be spread over more users.

State often argues in interagency meetings that cost increases are largely uncontrollable due to fluctuating exchange rates, local inflation, security costs, moves into new embassy compounds, and a variety of other extenuating factors. All of these arguments plausibly explain away cost escalations under the existing ways of doing business. USAID believes that the solution is to formulate new ways of doing business and set ambitious targets for cutting costs. The Department of Homeland Security was correct when it told GAO that individual cost savings initiatives at posts, such as replacing light bulbs, result in only marginal cost savings. Non-State customer agencies pushed State at the December 2011 ICASS Executive Board meeting to set numeric cost cutting targets. These customer agencies, including USAID, believe that such a proactive approach forces action more rapidly and is necessary to lower costs. Doing things the same way as usual is unsustainable and will inevitably result in agencies reducing their presence overseas, not because of an examination of their role in executing foreign policy, but because they have been priced out of business.

Alternate Service Providers (ASP): USAID agrees that there is potential to reduce costs by having other agencies step forward as alternate service providers. USAID's capacity to do so is constrained owing to the transfer of many of its administrative personnel to ICASS during earlier consolidation initiatives. Nevertheless, the JMB agreed in principle that it is open to USAID expanding its ASPs while providing appropriate attention to security concerns among a diverse customer base. This agreement could result in a marginal increase of ASPs but USAID does not foresee this as a "game changer."

- 5 -

<u>Uniform Service Standards</u>: GAO noted that State management counselors in Nairobi and Kigali indicated "that achieving uniform service standards does not necessarily constitute acceptable performance for many of their customers." USAID firmly agrees and urges an immediate assessment of the current service standards to determine their adequacy. This applies to motor pool services for "out of town" trips but also to other key service areas. This assessment should include a great deal of customer input; however, State asserts that the current standards do include customer input. USAID believes that the process for developing current standards resulted in the preeminence of service provider views and that State should embrace efforts to seek meaningful *customer* input when the standards are reassessed.

<u>General Observations</u>: State should be commended for taking several positive steps to improve services, lower costs, and establish metrics for performance. None of these were easy undertakings and no doubt there were a lot of internal stakeholders who had to be convinced to accept these changes. We believe now is an appropriate time for State to step up its efforts to another level by making major changes in its way of doing business and to hold key managers accountable for implementing the changes rapidly. USAID believes that the quicker State moves the more likely other customer agencies will turn to ICASS as the service provider of choice, thus eliminating duplicate support services and lowering costs to the U.S. Government.

Appendix VII: Comments from the Department of Commerce

Note: GAO comments
supplementing those in
the report text appear at
the end of this appendix.

UNITED STATES DEPARTMENT OF COMMERCE
The Under Secretary for International Trade
Washington, D.C. 20230

JAN 2 4 2012

Mr. Michael Courts
Acting Director, International Affairs and Trade
U.S. Government Accountability Office
Washington, DC 20548

Dear Mr. Courts:

Thank you for the opportunity to comment on the U.S. Government Accountability Office's (GAO) draft report titled, "Embassy Management: Agencies Missing Cost Saving Opportunities by Continuing to Duplicate Overseas Support Services" (GAO-12-317). The International Trade Administration (ITA) has been participating with the International Cooperative Administrative Support Services (ICASS) system since its inception and values the ICASS services immensely.

See comment 1.

We carefully reviewed the draft report, and agree with GAO that within the $2 billion ICASS operating budget, there is inefficiency and opportunities for improved productivity and cost savings. However, we disagree with the report's overall assertion that agencies continue to provide duplicative administrative services overseas. Much has happened since the 2004 GAO ICASS Audit within ITA in the areas of centralized and automated service delivery, requirements to reduce administrative overhead, and reduction in agency budgets.

Consistent with feedback we provided to GAO when they interviewed ITA staff, we offer five comments related to the draft report that, if considered, would likely improve customer satisfaction among non-State Department customers and reduce costs to individual agencies and the U.S. Government at large.

Thank you again for the opportunity to comment on the draft report. Enclosed are specific technical comments relating to the report.

Sincerely,

Francisco J. Sánchez

Enclosure

INTERNATIONAL
TRADE
ADMINISTRATION

Comments on GAO Draft Report 12-317: Agencies Mission Cost Savings Opportunities by Continuing to Duplicate Overseas Support Services

See comment 2.

Comment 1: ITA suggests that GAO recommend to Congress that the International Cooperative Administrative Support Services (ICASS) not be the provider of choice for any service that can be delivered remotely from the United States at a lower cost and with higher security than locally delivered ICASS services. The report identifies numerous examples of services being provided domestically at lower costs and higher quality, yet the draft GAO report paints this strategy as one that diminishes the cost effectiveness of ICASS.

See comment 3.

Comment 2: ITA questions the rationale underlying the GAO recommendation for mandatory participation in ICASS, particularly with only narrow exceptions. One of the proposed exceptions focuses on the overall costs to the U.S. Government, which could set a standard potentially impossible for any agency to meet.

ICASS was intended to be a voluntary system for the various reasons noted in the draft report. Each agency's objective is to steward its resources in the most effective manner possible to perform its mission. If similar services are available elsewhere at less cost than through ICASS and an agency chooses to "outsource" the service, then that agency is fulfilling its fiduciary responsibility to contain costs. The overall impact on the U.S. Government may be difficult to assess and hypothetical, but the cost savings to that agency are concrete and measurable.

While we agree that the potential for economies of scale may exist, the impact on overall U.S. Government costs are unclear. Human resource services for U.S. direct hires is an example of when mandatory use of ICASS likely would not result in efficiencies because of the differences in individual agency personnel policies. The agencies operating at each post are in the best position to make a case-by-case determination on what best meets each agency's needs to most effectively and efficiently accomplish its mission within its budgetary constraints.

See comment 4.

Comment 3: ITA suggests that GAO recommend that ICASS re-price its services to make buying larger bundles of services more appealing to customers and become more flexible, and allow customers to add and subtract services more quickly — cafeteria style — as customers needs change as they do from time to time in ITA.

Comment 4: ITA suggests that the GAO report focus more on the five lines found on page 17 where GAO comments that State has made little progress on cost containment efforts. This is monumentally important from a customer perspective where numerous OMB directives (i.e., OMB-10-19 "Fiscal Year 2012 Budget Guidance" and OMB-10-20 "Identifying Low-Priority Agency Programs") have focused on eliminating waste and increasing efficiency, as well as the recently published Executive Order 13589 (November 2011-Promoting Efficient Spending), which has directed agencies to promote more efficient spending. If ICASS were to embrace cost

See comment 5.

savings with the vigor that its customers have, it is likely that the ICASS operating budget would be much less that the $2 billion referenced in the report. Furthermore, on page 28 of the draft report, GAO highlights six ICASS services that fail in meeting their performance standards more often than meeting them. This level of underperformance deserves significant attention in light of the previously mentioned President's Executive Order, yet it garners no more than a few words in the last sentence of the draft report.

Comment 5: In multiple areas within the draft report GAO cites that they were unable to calculate savings that would accrue if more agencies joined ICASS. Conversely, GAO was also unable to verify the calculations of savings claimed by agencies that withdrew from ICASS. However, GAO still concluded that Congress may want to act to require agencies to participate in ICASS. In the absence of empirical data supporting ICASS as the most economical service delivery mechanism, ITA would suggest that GAO recommend the design of an evaluative model that would determine the cost effectiveness of either the ICASS cost or the proposals set forth by individual agencies. This type of recommendation would preclude a repeat of the 2004 and 2012 GAO studies that simply lament the lack of an empirical basis for ICASS decisions.

The following are GAO's comments on the Department of Commerce's letter dated January 24, 2012.

GAO Comments

1. Our analysis of ICASS data and observations in the field revealed clear instances of duplication of administrative services at overseas posts. Not all instances of nonparticipation in ICASS services indicate duplication, as we note in our report. However, because customer agencies have not justified their decisions to opt out of ICASS services, we could not determine which services obtained outside of ICASS were not duplicative.

2. We disagree. Our report notes that customer agencies may have valid reasons for opting out of ICASS services, including agencies' ability to obtain some services from their headquarters more efficiently or effectively than through ICASS. We do not suggest that this decision diminished the cost effectiveness of ICASS. However, we note that agencies typically do not provide justifications for these decisions, potentially limiting other customer agencies' ability to take advantage of these opportunities.

3. Our report suggests that Congress may wish to consider requiring agencies to participate in ICASS services unless they provide a business case to show that they can obtain these services outside of ICASS without increasing overall costs to the U.S. government or that their mission cannot be achieved within ICASS. We do not believe that these are narrow exceptions. However, we do believe that customer agencies should be required to collect, analyze, and present data to support their decisions to opt out of ICASS services. Without a rigorous analysis, agencies cannot demonstrate that their decisions do not negatively impact overall costs to the U.S. government.

4. The pricing of ICASS services was outside of the scope of our review.

5. ITA has misinterpreted the information presented in our draft report. Table 8 shows six selected ICASS services and their uniform service standards; however, this table shows that all six services have met their standard more often than not, doing so from about 59 to 74 percent of the time. Nevertheless, we agree that there is significant room for improvement in meeting established service standards.

6. Our report notes that we were unable to quantify the cost savings resulting from increased participation in ICASS because cost data on services outside ICASS are generally not comparable with ICASS cost data. However, our analysis of ICASS cost data shows that there

are significant economies of scale within ICASS, so costs to existing
customers would decrease as participation increases.

Appendix VIII: Comments from the Department of Agriculture

Note: GAO comments supplementing those in the report text appear at the end of this appendix.

United States
Department of
Agriculture

Farm and Foreign
Agricultural
Services

Foreign
Agricultural
Service

1400 Independence
Ave, SW
Stop 1001
Washington, DC
20250-1001

Mr. Michael J. Courts
Director, International Affairs and Trade
United States Government Accountability Office
441 G Street, N.W.
Washington, D.C. 20548

JAN 2 4 2012

Dear Mr. Courts:

The U.S. Department of Agriculture (USDA) appreciates this opportunity to respond to the Government Accountability Office (GAO) draft report "Embassy Management: Agencies Missing Cost Saving Opportunities by Continuing to Duplicate Overseas Support Services" (GAO-12-317).

One of the main points presented in the draft report is the lack of exclusive participation by agencies in the uniform International Cooperative Administrative Support Services (ICASS) system cost centers that are provided by the Department of State. However, USDA believes that 100 percent participation in ICASS is unattainable due to the wide variance of mission objectives and requirements that exist between government agencies. As GAO acknowledges in this draft report, even within the Department of State, entities cannot limit their procurement of necessary support services to ICASS cost centers alone. Individual agencies must have the flexibility to select services that best meet their particular needs.

The GAO recommendation that agencies provide a compelling business case justification before being allowed to obtain services outside of ICASS would impose a new burden that may be difficult to meet. Since ICASS is a cost distribution system, the actual cost to subscribe to any of its services is not able to be determined with any certainty in out-years. In the instances where ICASS superiority over other options is not clear (and absent any mitigating mission-specific considerations as discussed above), USDA's current practice is to commit to the service whose cost-benefit is guaranteed. For example, this has led USDA to leverage its existing infrastructure in Washington to support overseas operations in areas such as travel, financial management, procurement, and the payment of local vendors and Foreign Officers' entitlements. The GAO recommendations would disrupt this practice by mandating that USDA commit to generic ICASS services at unknown cost even when tailored alternatives at fixed rates are available. While USDA concurs with the GAO observation that data supporting the assumed cost savings of such arrangements has been difficult to quantify, we do not conclude that the savings are not valid or justified.

Sincerely,

Suzanne Heinen
Acting Administrator
Foreign Agricultural Service

See comment 1.

The following are GAO's comments on the Department of Agriculture's letter dated January 24, 2012.

GAO Comments

1. Our Matter for Congressional Consideration contains language that gives the agencies the flexibility to opt out of ICASS services when they can provide a business case to show that they can obtain these services outside of ICASS without increasing overall costs to the U.S. government. While we found that agencies generally are not developing these analyses, our report notes that agencies may have valid reasons for not participating in specific ICASS services. We also note that, without comparable data on costs, ICASS management is poorly positioned to convince agencies that participation in ICASS services is in their own interest. As a result, we believe both customer agencies and ICASS management are responsible for collecting and sharing cost data to ensure that customer agencies are making informed decisions on whether or not to participate in ICASS services. We believe that if conducted in close coordination with the ICASS Service Center and other participating agencies, preparing business cases need not be overly burdensome and could lead to significant, long term savings for the U.S. government that would justify the additional effort.

Appendix IX: Comments from the Department of Homeland Security

Note: GAO comments supplementing those in the report text appear at the end of this appendix.

U.S. Department of Homeland Security
Washington, DC 20528

Homeland
Security

January 26, 2012

Michael Courts
Director, Homeland Security and Justice
U.S. Government Accountability Office
441 G Street, NW
Washington, DC 20548

Re: Draft Report GAO-12-317: "EMBASSY MANAGEMENT: Agencies Missing Cost
    Savings Opportunities by Continuing to Duplicate Overseas Support Services"

Dear Mr. Courts,

Thank you for the opportunity to review and comment on this draft report. The U.S. Department of Homeland Security (DHS) appreciates the U.S. Government Accountability Office's work in planning and conducting its review and issuing this report.

While the report did not recommend management action for DHS, we do not agree with recommendations contained in the draft report that have direct implications for the Department.

Overseas posts are critical to our mission. DHS works closely with international partners, including foreign governments, major multilateral organizations, and global businesses, to strengthen the security of the networks of global trade and travel, upon which our Nation's economy and communities rely. Today, DHS is in virtually every corner of the world, with 11 Components and over 1,400 personnel stationed in more than 75 countries.

Since its inception in 2003, DHS and its Components have utilized the International Cooperative Administrative Support Services (ICASS) system provided by the U.S. Department of State. We are concerned that the recommendations in the draft report, related to ICASS services, may hinder our overseas operations and increase costs, while at the same time not fully addressing opportunities to maximize efficiencies within the ICASS system.

See comment 1.

Specifically, we do not agree with GAO's recommendation to make all ICASS services mandatory at all overseas locations. The draft report recommends that "Congress may wish to consider requiring agencies to participate in ICASS services" and to 'opt out' of an ICASS cost center, the agency must "provide a business case to show that they can obtain these services outside of ICASS without increasing overall costs to the U.S. government or that their mission cannot be achieved within ICASS."

See comment 2.

While DHS fully supports the realization of any significant cost savings possible related to U.S. government overseas and/or ICASS system operations, it is unclear if mandatory use of the current ICASS system will decrease costs. GAO's review of ICASS did not fully consider that the data over time showed increased participation had led to increased total costs to provide any given service. Specifically, GAO's review looked at each cost center independently and, in doing so, did not recognize that an increase in demand has a corollary impact on other cost centers, such as procurement, building operating expenses, and security. In other words, as more services are provided, additional personnel and infrastructure are required, thus increasing total service costs. Consequently, greater participation in ICASS may not necessarily reduce costs to the government. The solution to the growth of ICASS costs is not to mandate that ICASS grow even more, but that serious consideration be given to a leaner, smaller, more efficient ICASS.

See comment 3.

In making its recommendation, it appears GAO has incorrectly assumed that all U.S. agencies overseas are co-located within U.S. embassies or consulates and, therefore, can easily use ICASS services provided there. To the contrary, DHS personnel are often posted in airports, seaports, or other locations located far away from embassies or consulates. For example, of the U. S. Customs and Border Protection's approximately 400 employees in Canada, only 4 work inside the confines of an embassy or consulate. The others are located at airport locations, where services, such as office space, are provided by the host government. As a result, these personnel benefit little from ICASS services, such as photocopying and motor pool services, offered at embassies or consulates.

See comment 4.

In addition, GAO asserts that "agencies are providing potentially duplicative services at posts overseas." However, GAO does not differentiate between duplicative services provided by an agency at post and services provided from the United States to an agency at post. DHS believes it is important to make a distinction between Foreign Service agencies, which often self-provide services using a cadre of personnel based at post, and an agency like DHS, which largely self-provides services using domestic-based personnel. In the latter example, DHS support staff (hired mainly to provide services for *domestic* operations) perform a dual role in also providing support to DHS personnel based *abroad*. For example, many DHS overseas administrative functions are supported by domestic databases, such as time and attendance, payroll, personnel, budget formulation, budget execution, and accounting. It is important to recognize the potential cost savings to the government of not paying for services abroad that are already being provided 'at home.'

Again, thank you for the opportunity to review and comment on this draft report. Technical and sensitivity comments were previously provided under separate cover. We look forward to working with you on future Homeland Security issues.

Sincerely,

Jim H. Crumpacker
Director
Departmental GAO-OIG Liaison Office

2

The following are GAO's comments on the Department of Agriculture's letter dated January 24, 2012.

GAO Comments

1. Our Matter for Congressional Consideration contains language that gives the agencies flexibility to opt out of ICASS services in cases where agencies are unable to meet their missions using those services. We believe that requiring agencies to develop business cases to justify their decisions to opt out of ICASS services will ensure that that are making decisions based on hard data and facts, rather than on poorly supported perception of cost and quality.

2. We disagree. We examined how ICASS unit costs are related to the level of services provided controlling for the year of the service, the region where the post is located, and whether the posts are standard or "lite" posts. We used data from 2000 to 2010, which reflect the increasing overall ICASS cost. We found strong evidence that unit cost decreases as the level of services increases despite increasing overall ICASS cost over the years. We looked at the cost centers independently and together, and the findings on the relationship between unit cost and the level of services are consistent.

3. Again, our Matter for Congressional Consideration contains language that gives the agencies flexibility to opt out of ICASS services in cases where agencies are unable to meet their missions using those services. In cases where DHS personnel are located far away from embassies or consulates, DHS should be able to develop a simple business case to explain its decision not to participate in ICASS services.

4. Our analysis of ICASS data and observations in the field revealed clear instances of duplication of administrative services at overseas posts. Not all instances of nonparticipation in ICASS services indicate duplication, as we note in our report. For example, we note that in some instances, nonparticipation may indicate that a service is not offered to all agencies at a post or that an agency does not need a particular service. We also noted instances where agency officials indicated that they were able to obtain some services from their headquarters more efficiently or effectively than through ICASS. In such instances, nonparticipation does not necessarily indicate duplication of services. However, because customer agencies have not justified their decisions to opt out of ICASS services, we could not determine which services obtained outside of ICASS were not duplicative.

Appendix X: GAO Contact and Staff Acknowledgments

GAO Contact	Michael Courts, (202) 512-8980 or courtsm@gao.gov
Staff Acknowledgments	In addition to the contact listed above, Jacquelyn Williams-Bridgers, Jess Ford, James Michels, Robert Ball, Ming Chen, Christopher Mulkins, Kyerion Printup, James Ashley, Richard Brown, Christina Bruff, David Dayton, Martin de Alteriis, Fang He, Jill Lacey, Grace Lui, Amanda Miller, Karen O'Conor, and Christina Werth made major contributions to this report.